nows what it takes to be a champion. No matter what
you're involved in or what your stage of life is, I guaran-
'll be encouraged and equipped as Ryan helps you have
spective and confidence to fight *from* victory and not *for*

—**Lon Williams,** pastor, Liberty Church

deep admiration for Ryan and his approach to his profes-
d life. He does a great job of unpacking the big picture and
ng fully engaged in the mile he is in. Get ready to run the
your life.

—**Eric Johnson,** author, speaker, pastor,
Bethel Church, Redding, CA

ook will inspire you to chase bigger dreams, challenge you
ink success, and invite you into a deeper relationship with
yan shares with incredible vulnerability that we can draw
to God both on the mountain tops and in the valleys.

—**Michael Chitwood,** Executive Director of Church
and Ministry Partnerships, World Vision

Run the Mile You're In is not about wi
running records. It's about always movii
ward is an act of courage. The reward i
embracing the dream.

—**Bart Yasso**, newly retired chief runr

Ryan's journey on and off the course is t
ful way to live by helping others. This is
and finding your sense of purpose.

—**Meb Keflezighi**, Olymp
Marathon and I

What I love about this book is that we ge
Hall. He talks about why it wasn't just th
to his athletic and life success but also his
world's most competitive sport takes so
all in this fine new book.

—**Bill Rodgers**, four tii
N

Ryan examines and deciphers his well-liv
not you share his deep Christian faith, the
He says that he always strove to run free
book contains many lessons to help you f

—**Amby Burfoot**, 1968 B
writer, *Runner's* \

I'm inspired by so many of the chapte
"Vision," because the "genius is seeing it ir
because we can accomplish anything if w
the sacrifices involved. "Failure," because v
try. And "Faith," because with faith, nothi
vividly drives home these and many other

—**Dave McGillivray**, DMS

Ryan
career
tee yc
the pe
victor

I have
sion a
yet be
race c

This
to ret
God.
neare

RUN THE
MILE
YOU'RE
IN

RUN THE
MILE
YOU'RE
IN

FINDING GOD IN EVERY STEP

RYAN HALL

ZONDERVAN

Run the Mile You're In
Copyright © 2019 by Ryan Hall

ISBN 978-0-310-35444-4 (audio)

Requests for information should be addressed to:
Zondervan, *3900 Sparks Dr. SE, Grand Rapids, Michigan 49546*

Library of Congress Cataloging-in-Publication Data

Names: Hall, Ryan, 1982- author.
Title: Run the mile you're in : finding God in every step / Ryan Hall.
Description: Grand Rapids, Michigan : Zondervan, [2019] |
Identifiers: LCCN 2018052330 (print) | LCCN 2019004481 (ebook) |
    ISBN 9780310354390 (ebook) | ISBN 9780310354376 (hardcover)
Subjects: LCSH: Hall, Ryan, 1982- | Long-distance runners—United
    States—Biography. | Running—Religious aspects—Christianity.
Classification: LCC GV1061.15.H35 (ebook) | LCC GV1061.15.H35 A3 2019
    (print) | DDC 796.42092 [B] —dc23
LC record available at https://lccn.loc.gov/2018052330

Author is represented by the literary agency of The Fedd Agency, Inc., P.O. Box 341973, Austin, Texas 78734.

Interior design: Denise Froehlich
Cover design: Curt Diepenhorst
Cover photo: World Marathon Challenge

Printed in the United States of America

18 19 20 21 22 /LSC/ 10 9 8 7 6 5 4 3 2 1

This book is dedicated to my wife, Sara, for always believing in me and supporting me; to my kids, who have added so much joy to my life and will be the greatest legacy I could leave; to my extended family, who was on this journey with me through the ups and downs; to my friends who encouraged me along the way; and to everyone who is on the journey of discovering what God has put inside of them.

Contents

Acknowledgments

I'd like to acknowledge Tom Dean, VP of Marketing at Zondervan, for reaching out to me to consider writing a book to share my story. Without his prompting, this book never would have happened. I'd also like to acknowledge my friend Pastor Matthew Barnett, who pastors the Dream Center in Los Angeles and took me on the craziest weeklong adventure of my life, and connected me with the wonderful people at The Fedd Agency to make this book become a reality. And to the wonderful staff at Zondervan, thanks for helping turn a runner into an author through some serious editing throughout the process. Writing a book is like running a marathon. There may be only one person out there running the race or writing the book, but there is a huge team behind that person, which makes all the difference. Thanks to my team who "ran the race" with me.

Vision

I remember the image vividly—the sparkling bright blue water of Big Bear Lake in the high mountain region of Southern California. Because I'd grown up in these mountains, I'd taken in this image often, but this time it was accompanied by a vision. I was a thirteen-year-old eighth-grade basketball player—one who seemed to be stuck at four foot eleven and ninety-nine pounds—and despite being one of the hardest workers on the team, I wasn't seeing much playing time. But that didn't keep me from enjoying being a part of the team and observing our weekly games from the sidelines. On this particular winter travel trip, the van was full of rambunctious junior high boy energy, the kind that would give most adults a headache, but I found myself tuning out the chaos and gazing at Big Bear Lake. It was as if all the commotion couldn't penetrate my ears; all I could hear was God giving me a desire I'd never had before. I felt like He was giving me the aspiration to run around the lake. The desire wasn't overly obvious; it was more as if I had an itch that could be relieved only by attempting the feat.

Looking back, I realize that my experience in the van was

a God-inspired vision, though at the time it seemed like simply an idea that popped into my head. Like many boys, I'd grown up mad about sports and had played the big three American favorites: basketball, football, and—my biggest love—baseball. The son of a former drafted major league baseball player, I dreamed of one day following in my dad's footsteps and getting drafted by a major league team. I spent a considerable amount of time pursuing this dream, tirelessly throwing a baseball into a green tarp with a painted white box that signified the strike zone. Always one to help me fulfill my dreams, my dad had created this pitching practice setup in our back yard.

Yet my vision in the van wasn't about baseball. It wasn't even about football or basketball. It was about *running*. This came as a surprise to me because I'd had zero interest in the sport. I'd been around 5K road races and had watched my dad compete in marathons, but I didn't have any desire to run. Running seemed boring and, well, kind of pointless. Why would you choose a sport, like track, where you run around in circles as fast as you can only to finish in the same spot where you started?

Thankfully, though, I paid attention to the voice urging me to run around Big Bear Lake. But my vision wasn't an easy one to live out. The only running I'd done was short sprints on the basketball court, the football field, or the baseball diamond. And here's the kicker: it's fifteen miles around the lake. Fifteen miles is challenging enough, but the lake is also at seven thousand feet altitude. The thin air at that elevation makes you feel like you're breathing through a straw. Despite those obstacles, something about this crazy vision captured me.

It's easy to dismiss the visions that pop into our minds, especially when they don't seem to fit with the rest of our lives. I'd dreamed of becoming a major league baseball player, not a runner. And it was just a sudden desire I had—*I want to run around Big Bear Lake.* I hadn't heard an audible voice from God. I hadn't read anything etched in stone. I hadn't received a prophetic word. But I felt a strong pull in my heart, a passion to do something I'd never before imagined, and so it seemed important to act on my vision.

It's crazy how sometimes our smallest decisions turn out to have the most significant consequences. We spend hours and hours writing lists of pros and cons and seeking advice from friends, family members, and colleagues about the big decisions—where to go to college, whether to get married or have kids, which job offer to accept—but we rarely deliberate the small decisions. We tell ourselves that those little things don't matter when actually they can be extremely important.

I'm not saying that the big decisions shouldn't be carefully considered, but I've learned that we also shouldn't dismiss the small ones, because these decisions can subtly change the trajectory of our lives. If I hadn't acted on my God-given vision to run around the lake, I never would have had the opportunity to run at Stanford, meet my wife, compete on two Olympic teams, travel around the globe, and live out all the amazing experiences I've had as a result of running. And all of this came from a God-inspired seedling of a thought, one that I could have easily dismissed. I am so grateful I didn't.

After that road trip with the basketball team, I shared my vision with my dad. I'm surprised he didn't dismiss it right away as being crazy and not a good idea. Now that I'm a dad, I'm not sure I would have reacted the way he did. I would have been more likely to tell any of my four daughters that she should start with a smaller, more attainable goal. But that's not how my dad responded. He simply told me that if I wanted to run the fifteen miles around the lake, he would run it with me.

The more I look back on this, the more amazing his response seems. I tend to find myself wanting to give my kids advice and guidance, and there's certainly a place for that in parenting, but sometimes I need to take the dad hat off and partner with my kids' deepest desires. I need to say, "If that's what you want to do, let's do it together." I've learned a lot about God as I've increasingly viewed Him as the ultimate Father. Jesus describes God that way when He talks about how on earth, evil fathers know how to give good gifts to their kids; therefore, how much more does God, who is in heaven, know how to give good gifts to His kids (Matt. 7:11)? As I think about how I want to grow as a good father, I realize that I am interested in what my kids are into, and I do everything I can to support and help them in their dreams and journeys. How much more must God be interested in the desires of our hearts and in our dreams, especially if He is the one who put those dreams there to begin with? I really believe that God is intensely interested in our hearts and all the desires and dreams that reside in them as He leads us to chase after them.

The following Saturday morning, without any preparation, I laced up my high-top basketball shoes—hours later, my bulging blisters showed me that basketball shoes are a little different from running shoes—and headed out the door with my dad for what turned out to be a very long and painful run around Big Bear Lake. Before beginning our journey, my dad and I completed some light stretching on our front porch, then Dad had me pump my hand into a fist and then flat as fast as I could for one minute to show me how strong my heart had to be to pump blood throughout my body my entire life. (If you want to try it, be ready for some serious cramping and pain by the end of the minute.) He had me do this to show me that running was a way for me to make my heart stronger.

We then began the run with a walk, which became my custom throughout my running career, of about 100 meters as a way to warm the body up before beginning a slow jog. As a nonrunner, I understood that I was in for a major physical challenge, but I was not mentally prepared for it. I made it about six miles before we had to stop as we reached the dam and took a little time to watch some fishermen bait-fish in the deep blue waters. I've never enjoyed watching fishing so much in my entire life. I relished every second, hoping to postpone my run as long as possible. Starting back up after that brief break, my quads felt like jello, and I wasn't even halfway there yet! I questioned whether I could make it the last nine miles. Luckily, I had already navigated the hilliest section of the paved, well-traveled road looping the lake. That was the only factor in my favor at that point.

Three miles later, we stopped at a liquor store to grab a cold Sobe to replenish my depleted body of hydration, sugar, and electrolytes. The icy, sugary, orange-carrot drink tasted divine in my fatigued and dehydrated state. Once again, it was challenging to start running again after taking a break. Yet somehow I found a way to keep putting one foot in front of the other, in large part because of my dad's support. An avid runner who could knock off fifteen miles in half the time it was going to take the two of us, he never let on whether he was impatient or bored. My dad just stayed by my side offering encouragement after encouragement and telling me how great I was doing. I definitely didn't feel like I was doing great, but hearing those positive words went a long way in helping me maintain a hopeful, confident belief that I would finish the full run.

Our last stop was with 1.5 miles to go. I was hurting worse than I had ever hurt in my life, and I can imagine that I looked even worse than I felt. My dad decided it would be good for me to take a little break and ice my legs in the frigid lake water, which must have been colder than 50 degrees in the winter. I didn't care how cold the lake was; I had lost feeling in my legs miles ago. After icing our legs for about ten minutes, I shoved my blistered, battered feet into my basketball shoes, laced them up, and set off on the longest 1.5 miles of my life. I felt as heavy as an elephant. With every step, it felt like it took great strength and energy to lift my foot off the ground.

When we finally made it home, I was beyond exhausted. I remember stumbling through the front door and being faced with the runner's debate: couch or refrigerator? I couldn't decide whether I was more tired or hungry, but I ended up opting for the couch. In my exhausted state, I suddenly found it was a lot easier to connect with God. I didn't have to go into my prayer closet and put earplugs in and beg God to let me hear His voice. It was more as if my immense fatigue had quieted my mind and all of the distractions around me and the only thing left was His voice. Until this point, I knew who God was. I occasionally spent a little time reading the Bible and praying, but I wouldn't say I was conversational with God. But I discovered that when I am exhausted, I can more easily pray and—more important— hear His voice. Depleted from my journey, I felt God speak to the depths of my heart for the first time in my life. And what He told me was nothing short of amazing. God unleashed His purpose for the next season of my life. God spoke to me that I would one day run with the best runners in the world and that I would also be given the gift of helping others through my running. Now, I knew what running with the best runners in the world looked like: the Olympics. But helping people through running? It took ten years before I discovered how powerful my running could be as a way to love others.

Purpose

It was acting on my vision to run around the lake that led to God's revealing His purpose for my next season of life. If I had not had the vision before the purpose, I wouldn't have believed the purpose was accurate or possible. Something activated within me on that run around the lake. Somehow, despite the pain and my dread toward running, I became intrigued with it. I began to see potential in myself I hadn't seen before. There began an inkling of curiosity to see why God had given me the vision and desire to run around the lake. After that moment with God on the couch, everything changed. I no longer saw my purpose as one day playing professional baseball. My purpose, on my way to running with the best guys in the world and loving others through running, was to run and nurture the talent God had put inside of me. Not only did what I do change but also who I was changed. I went from a typical middle school boy dabbling in this and that, trying to be cool and just get by in school, to a driven, disciplined, and focused athlete. I never lived my life the same way again. My goals changed. My desires changed. My friends changed. How I went about my life and how I spent my time changed.

That day I began an adventure with God that lasted twenty years before it evolved into a new season of life.

People often ask me if I was surprised to make Olympic teams and set American records, and my answer is always no because God told me where I was going from the very beginning. That day, God gave me a belief that I was designed for a mission. One of my favorite movies is *I, Robot* for the reason that at the climax of the movie (spoiler alert), the main character, a robot named Sonny, realizes that his creator (a scientist) designed him to help save the world. Once Sonny realizes his purpose, he is able to carry out his mission because he realizes that his designer gave him everything he needed to fulfill it when he created him. In the same way, I believe that we each have a mission to accomplish and that we have been designed in such a way that we are not lacking anything to accomplish it. Everything we need is already inside of us. We just have to find it and figure out how to cultivate it.

Having purpose is important because the road is hard. My purpose sustained me through years and years of gut-wrenching lows, disappointments, and heartache. My purpose gave me the courage to get back up every time I stumbled, because I knew I hadn't yet lived out the mission I was designed to carry out. It's as if my purpose was calling me forward, like a magnet pulling me toward accomplishing what I needed to when my strength was weak.

I believe that God has given all of us a purpose, a calling, a mission—whatever terminology you prefer. He has given each of us our own promised land to enter the same way He created the Promised Land for Israel to enter. He might not have communicated our purpose through an audible voice, a flash of lightning, or a vivid vision, but because God is the ultimate Father, I believe that He wants to show us what we were created for more than we want to find it, so He is going to reveal to us that purpose. Our job is simply to watch for it and act on it.

Sometimes God ignites a dead desire within us. At other times, he gives us a set of skills and abilities that allows us to do something only we could do, as was the case for Sonny in *I, Robot*. I know Sonny is just a character in a movie, but I have felt the same sensation. When I found what I was created to do, suddenly my life made sense and what seemed impossible became possible. God created us to go after the seemingly impossible because He designed us with a purpose in mind! Ephesians 2:10 says, "For we are His workmanship, created in Christ Jesus for good works, which God prepared beforehand so that we would walk in them."

Maybe you already know what you were created to do. Maybe you haven't yet discovered your purpose. Or maybe your purpose in one season of your life is shifting to a different purpose in a new season. It may take some dialogue with God—and with people in your life—to figure out what He has created you to do. I am now in a season of figuring out what's in the next season after retiring from professional running a little more than three years ago. I'm not sure what my next mission is, but I know that the end of one mission signifies the beginning of another. I know that God has something else for me to go after, something He probably had been preparing me for in my last season of life as a professional runner. I'm beginning to see that coaching others to achieve their goals in running brings life to me in much the same way that competing did, and I can see that perhaps all throughout my professional running career, God was preparing me to coach. As a result, I have begun to coach a few athletes, beginning with my wife and also helping to coach my daughter. I'm not sure where the road will take me, but I believe God always asks me to do my best with what is right in front of me, and so I'm continuing to love and help others through running. I am carrying on the purpose of the last season in a new way.

If you really want to discover the purpose for your season of life, I believe that one of the best ways to find it is to talk to others who know you well. Sometimes it's easier to see someone else's giftedness than your own. If you are searching for your next God-given mission, I encourage you to surround yourself with close friends who will tell you what gifts God has given you and what those gifts may be equipping you to do. My dad—who obviously knows me well—did an amazing job of telling me the potential he saw inside me without bending my arm to act on that potential. He knew it had to be my choice, that I needed to act on my own desire. Even before I began running, Dad used to tell me that I could be a great runner if I wanted to be. Yet he always followed that comment with, "But you have to be the one who wants to run." I'm so glad he didn't push me into running, because if he had, I would have been doing it for him and likely would have quit after my first significant setback. Passion that comes from our own drive is so much more powerful than passion derived from another person's dreams.

A few years ago, I coached high school cross-country at my oldest daughter's school, University Preparatory School in Redding, California. Coaching has made me realize how different my life would have been had I not received the purpose I was created for when I was thirteen years old. I imagine my desire to fit in and be cool would have led to some poor choices that would have had negative consequences on what colleges I could have attended, who I would have surrounded myself with, and ultimately, what I would do with my life.

Because of that, as a coach, my primary goal is to help my athletes find purpose for their lives—whether it be running or something different. I am learning to do this by using the same approach my dad used with me. I "call out the gold" in them. I let my athletes know what could be possible for them, but ultimately, I allow them to decide whether they want to pursue their potential. For example, when I watch certain athletes run, I can tell by their stride, footspeed, and how they respond to training that they have an exceptional level of running talent, so I try to make sure they know what I am seeing rather than just keeping my belief in them hidden. It seems obvious that I should tell my athletes about the talent I see in them, but I've found that it takes intentionality for me to "call out the gold," because often my thoughts stay captive in my mind. Another way for me to help my athletes find their purpose is to take an interest in them as persons. I don't want just to talk running with them. I like to get to know their likes and dislikes, what they wake up in the morning excited about, what makes them tick, what motivates them, what they fear, and I just try to learn about them. Doing so, I learn a lot about how God created them and possibly what gifts He has given them to use, which allows me to help them find their purpose. There is no greater feeling for me as a coach than to help someone find their purpose, because I know firsthand how empowering it is to live a life of purpose. Once an athlete finds their purpose, they can focus their entire being on cultivating it.

When I think about Jesus and how He cultivated the purpose for which He came, I recall the passage in Matthew 16 where Peter rebukes Jesus for saying He would be delivered to the elders, chief priests, and scribes and then killed before being raised from the dead three days later. Jesus' response

RUN THE MILE YOU'RE IN

reveals His passion for fulfilling His purpose: "But He turned and said to Peter, 'Get behind Me, Satan! You are a stumbling block to Me; for you are not setting your mind on God's interests, but man's'" (Matt. 16:23).

It's hard not to laugh at the harshness of Jesus' response. Who calls their friend Satan? Seems kind of intense, right? But Jesus was so intent on doing what He had been put on earth to accomplish that He rightfully saw anything that challenged His mission as being from the devil. That's how focused I want to be on accomplishing what God created me to do, because I realize that today, more than ever, so many distractions pull me away from my mission. During my career as a professional runner, I didn't feel like just a runner on the starting line trying to run fast. I felt a clear and deep sense of purpose coupled with a strong vision of where I was going to end up. I really believe that it was this sense of vision that propelled me to greater heights than I otherwise could have attained, and I believe it is a key for all of us to fulfill our purpose.

Sacrifice

After my run around Big Bear Lake, I asked my dad to write me a training program for my running. Even though the sport Dad knew best was baseball, he had already coached some very good runners (one of whom ran 9:05 for two miles as a senior in high school) during his time as a teacher in both Australia and Seattle. He'd also read dozens of books about running and had developed into a good runner himself, running close to a sub-three-hour marathon, so he was well equipped to help me on my journey. He handwrote my training plan for a month at a time, and I followed it religiously. My first forty-mile week, when I was a freshman in high school, felt like such a huge accomplishment, which is pretty funny to reflect on now, considering that years later I would put in more than forty miles per week when I was tapering (resting) for a race.

That's what progressive training is all about, though—increasing your normal. When you are accustomed to running twenty or thirty miles a week, a forty-mile week feels like a huge jump. Pretty soon, though, your body adapts and gets stronger to the point where what was once a challenge has now become easy. The principle is simple: once the body adapts to a new normal, you need to adjust your training to stretch yourself again, which will cause you to get even stronger.

The body isn't the only thing that needs to adapt to increased training volume or intensity. An equally big step in becoming stronger is changing the way you think about your training. What you define as hard training will become hard training for you. As you train harder and harder, you must adjust your mind to believe that you aren't training as hard as it wants you to believe it is. That's why training in a group can be so powerful. When you train on your own, it's easy to convince yourself you are training very hard—until you find yourself with a group of people who are training much harder. Suddenly, your training regimen doesn't seem as impressive as you once thought, and you're willing to train even harder to challenge your body's ability to grow in endurance.

After retiring from professional running, I attempted to complete an event called the World Marathon Challenge—running seven marathons in seven days on seven continents. In my training for the Challenge, I hadn't run farther than eight miles in practice for a long run, and my weekly mileage was around twenty miles a week. Considering the level of my training, the thought of running 26.2 miles a day for seven days was daunting, to say the least. But just prior to the competition, I received a copy of a book by an author who completed fifty Ironman triathlons in fifty days in fifty states. (An Ironman consists of swimming 2.4 miles, biking 112 miles, and running 26.2 miles.) You can imagine that reading about the author's challenge put my own in perspective! All of a sudden, my challenge seemed a lot more doable, even if I hadn't trained for it.

The beauty of sports—and of life—is that we get to

encourage each other to do what we once felt was impossible. Consider Roger Bannister, the first man to break four minutes in the mile. It took thousands of years for the first man to run a mile under four minutes, but after Bannister did it in 1954, it started a cascade of world records in the mile run. Today, the world record stands at 3:43, and one man has even run back-to-back miles at a sub-four-minute pace. Today, it's fairly normal for an elite runner to clock a sub-four mile. To me, this is proof that once we cease to be impressed by the size of our challenges, our ability to overcome them grows exponentially.

Another thing I've had to learn to do when taking on major challenges is to borrow confidence from others. Over the course of my career, I trained with many other runners who were far better than me, but as I trained alongside them and became able to do the workouts and live the lifestyle they were living, I believed I could achieve what they had achieved. There is one catch to borrowing confidence from someone else: you must be able to rejoice in their successes. Often when one of my teammates or peers popped a big race, I got upset. It was as if their success meant my value took a dive. I had to remind myself to celebrate others' achievements because what makes me special, important, or of worth has nothing to do with my or anyone else's performance. I shouldn't look down on myself for not doing as well as someone else because the goal isn't to be better than everyone else. My goal, when I was at my best, was always to be the best version of me that I could be. I found that if I was inspired by the breakthrough of others, then often those breakthroughs became my catalyst for believing I could do it too and experiencing my own breakthroughs.

I had to borrow confidence quite a lot during my freshman

year of high school, since I had never trained or raced before. My dad and I continued to train together after school. I remember sharing the road on quite a few chilly, dark winter nights as my dad led me through interval sessions, fartleks (speed play in which you run hard and then easy in random intervals of time), and long runs. My dad's confidence in my fitness grew, and I drew from that confidence. It wasn't long before forty-mile weeks started to feel normal. I loved training and devoted myself to my new craft with everything I had. I wasn't racing at the time—just training for my freshman track season. I didn't run cross-country as a freshman because I didn't know that sport existed, because my high school was too small to have a cross-country program. Fortunately, my dad was a teacher at the high school and was able to start both the cross-country and track programs so I could compete. I recall sitting in a school board meeting with him as he successfully petitioned the school to begin those programs. Dad went on to coach multiple teams—as well as multiple individuals—to state titles, so it's safe to say the board was glad they decided to begin those programs.

Borrowing confidence from my dad and learning the mindset for training were certainly necessary and important at that stage in my development, but it wasn't until one of the most important events of my life happened that the door for me to achieve my God-given potential truly opened. I was still training for track like a madman, but I wasn't yet willing to let go of my childhood dream of playing professional baseball. I still believed I could do both sports well—and simultaneously. When I told my dad that I planned to go out for the high school baseball team, he gave me some wise advice: "You can be good at multiple things, but if your goal is to be great, you need to choose one." Those words hit home for me because I didn't want to be merely good at baseball or running. I wanted to be great, great in the sense of developing my running talent to its fullest expression. Still, even after that conversation, I couldn't quite shake the baseball bug. I went ahead and tried out for the high school team, but partway through the week, I saw how juggling two demanding activities diluted the energy I could bring to each. At the end of the weeklong baseball tryout, I told the coach that I had decided to run instead of play baseball, which the JV baseball coach seemed okay with. But it wasn't that simple.

The following week, while I was in math class, I got a message that the varsity baseball coach wanted to speak with me. Being the shy and timid freshman that I was, I started sweating. I reluctantly dragged myself to his classroom, having no idea what he wanted to speak to me about. The coach sat me down and told me I was making a mistake. He believed that I had some ability and could really help the team. In hindsight, I think he may have been recruiting my dad more than me, knowing that if I played baseball, my dad would likely help coach the pitchers, which is something he'd done in previous years that had benefitted the team greatly.

I'd gotten to know the baseball coach fairly well through my dad, so I nodded in agreement throughout the entire conversation and convinced myself that the coach—whom I really liked—was right. He closed our talk by telling me that one day we would both look back and be glad we'd had this conversation. The truth is, to this day I am glad we had that discussion. Not because I went on to play professional baseball but because, as soon as I sat back down in math class, I knew, for the first time, without a doubt, that playing baseball wasn't the right decision. I realized that if I wanted to reach my full potential in running, I had to focus on it alone. And that's what I did.

Achieving our fullest potential in any endeavor requires focus, which is made possible only through sacrifice, because focusing completely on one thing requires that we take our eyes off everything else. We sacrifice what's going on in the periphery so that we can more clearly see what we are focused on. When I focused on running, I didn't just lose baseball. I instantly lost all of my friends too, because all of them were playing baseball, basketball, and football, and I wasn't participating in those sports anymore. Losing my friends was a sacrifice, but it was a sacrifice that God knew would be good for me. At that point—like many young teens—I was more concerned with having cool friends than having friends with good values, character, goals, and passions. Had I continued to hang out with my friends, I most likely would have gotten involved in the party scene and ended up on a dead-end path. Yet even the loneliness of losing my friends was something that God used for good.

Soon after I decided to focus on running, I often found myself alone. I would walk through the quad of my high school during lunchtime with nobody to hang out with, and instead of eating lunch with friends, I would go into my dad's classroom and play cribbage with him and his aide. As I walked through the quad one day, I said a silent prayer to God. I told Him that because I didn't have any friends, I needed God to be my friend. It was in this loneliness that my faith went from a belief in God to a relationship with Him. It was the beginning of a new friendship that lasted far beyond my days as a competitive runner.

I've come to learn that sacrifices seem like sacrifices only at the time you make them. Sacrifices are things God is calling us to give up for our own good. If you think about it, it's not really a sacrifice to act in a way that will improve yourself.

I like to look at sacrifice as a forest burning down. Fires are messy, dangerous, and even catastrophic. But they're essential for clearing the forest of dead underbrush and preparing it for new growth. All of us have things in our lives that need to be burned up so something new and beautiful can grow in their place. We just need to change how we see these sacrifices—from something we have to give up to something that is going to make us better people who are going to live out God's plans and purpose for us.

My sacrifice—the loss of other sports and the loss of my friends—influenced my training. I suddenly had a lot more time and energy to devote to my training. At this time, I was a big fan of the Rocky movies. I felt like I was living my own Rocky story—running up snowy mountains, splitting wood, and doing situps and pushups day after day. And it wasn't long before I started to reap the fruit of my sacrifice. The spring of my freshman year, my mile time improved from 5:32 to 4:30. More important, though, was the lesson I'd learned: the way to enter my God-given destiny is through the door of focus, which can be opened only with the key of sacrifice.

Goals

My dad and I began every summer with a ritual. We'd get a wheelbarrow, a couple of bags of cement, and a shovel, and we'd go into the back yard to pour a little cement slab. Before the cement dried, we'd write our goals for the year in it. It was Dad's way to get both of us to commit to going after our goals. But it was not so much about the result. It was, instead, the pursuit of those goals that mattered. Whatever we wrote in the wet cement, we committed to going after with all our hearts. And Dad was never disappointed if I didn't hit my goals. He was just proud that I had pursued them with everything I had.

In later years, our house flooded (ironically, that happened the day I set the American record in the half marathon) and was rebuilt, only to be gutted by a terrible fire and rebuilt again several years later. Yet that slab of cement remains, still proclaiming our goals. That's the power of writing your goals in a substance like cement—there's no erasing them, no going back on them, no forgetting them. It's a permanent record of your commitment.

Writing down my goals didn't stop with the cement slab. I wrote my goals on my school book covers, scribbled them in permanent marker on my walls, and even set clocks with dead batteries to the time I wanted to run for the mile. I posted a countdown until the next Olympics in my freshman dorm room at Stanford. Every morning when I woke up, I removed one day from the countdown to remind myself what I was going after and how many days of training I had left to make it happen.

As a goal-setting high-school runner, I was a huge fan of Jim Ryun, who had been the first high schooler to break four minutes in the mile and had gone on to set numerous world records in the mile and 800 meters as well as to win a silver medal at the 1968 Olympics in Mexico City. I admired Jim for what he had accomplished on the track, but I also admired him for his deep faith, which allowed him to endure the heartbreak of being tripped in the prelims of the 1,500 meters—the event he was favored to win—during the 1972 Munich Olympic Games. Jim's faith allowed him to view his misfortune as a way to relate to others and inspire them to get back up when they get knocked down. He went on to become a congressman for Kansas and has an annual summer running camp to inspire and teach high school runners. I wanted to follow in Jim's footsteps both as a runner and as a man of faith, so I set my goals to run the same times he had run when he was my age. The problem was I hadn't yet realized that we all progress in our own timing. Trying to mirror someone else's journey rarely works well, and it certainly didn't work well for me. Attempting to match Jim's high school times only led to my feeling frustrated, disappointed, and like I was failing.

I did accomplish some of those goals I wrote in cement—like running 4:30 for the 1,600 meters as a high school freshman and clocking the same distance in 4:05 as a junior. But I missed other goals—like running a 3:55 mile my senior year. In my last competition as a high schooler at the Maine Distance Festival, I gave the race everything I had but failed to break four minutes in the mile. I was devastated. I cooled down by myself, stopping in a grass field where I sat with tears flowing down my cheeks. My dreams and goals had been shattered. I'd heard the message so many times that if you work your hardest and truly believe, you will achieve your goals, but that hadn't happened. My pursuit had fallen far short.

Yes, for a few, hard work and belief will lead to the achievement of their goals. But if it's a goal that is not attainable, it won't be reached. A million kids might watch the Olympic Marathon on TV and all dream of one day winning the gold medal in that event. The truth is, though, no matter how much each of those million kids believes they will one day win Olympic gold and no matter how hard they train and no matter how perfectly they take care of their bodies, only one person can win that gold medal. The 999,999 others will be disappointed. I'll admit that this really bothers me. It doesn't seem fair that one can devote their entire life to the pursuit of their dream, doing everything in their power to attain it, only for the dream to end in heartbreaking disappointment.

I had given everything inside of me to achieve my goals in high school only to fall well short of them. And so I thought that maybe I had been pursuing the wrong goals. Maybe I shouldn't have been writing down how fast I wanted to run the mile but rather should have been going after something within my control. I was learning that as much as I wanted to will my body to do something, it might not be in the cards to actually do it.

During my sophomore year at Stanford, I dreamed of competing in both the 2004 Olympic Trials and Olympic Games. My pursuit of that goal ended with my little brother, Chad, and me driving our family's rusty blue van up to Sacramento to watch my girlfriend (now wife) compete in the track and field Olympic Trials. It was a memorable trip. On the way up, we had to stop every half hour or so because I'd come down with the flu and kept throwing up. After the ten-hour trek, Chad and I found a quiet spot down by the Sacramento River in which to park and get some sleep. We were "in a van, down by the river" for the next few days, living off tortillas, cold cheese, and Tapatio. Not exactly the Olympic dream I'd been pursuing for six years. I think most people can relate to the heartbreak I felt in that moment. When you give all you have to a goal or a pursuit, it's normal to feel an overwhelming sense of disappointment when it doesn't happen. But it's important not to get stuck there. That's not where the story ends. In this moment of pain, you need to take a hard look at your life and change your goals to something within your control.

The year following my unsuccessful Olympic bid, I stopped writing down my goals. I even ceased having performance goals at all because I knew, no matter how badly I wanted it, the result was partially out of my control. I shifted my focus from performance goals that I couldn't control to heart goals that I could control and live out every practice, every race, every day. I discovered that for me to perform at my highest level, I needed to believe that anything is possible with God—and that I could trust Him completely with the outcomes of my competitions—but that my focus needed to be not on my performance but instead on my heart. The Bible says, "Guard your heart above all else, for it determines the course of your life" (Prov. 4:23 NLT). I used to think that hard work determined the course of my life—and hard work definitely plays its part in success—but it is mainly my heart that determines where and how far I go in sports and in life.

It may seem counterintuitive to believe that heart goals are more powerful than performance goals, but I've experienced it to be true. Jesus was more passionate about people's hearts than about their behavior. Over and over, Jesus encouraged His followers to pay attention to their hearts. In Matthew 15:19, He says, "For out of the heart come evil thoughts, murders, adulteries, fornications, thefts, false witness, slanders." Jesus was making the point that if we want to change our actions, we need to change our hearts. It's the heart that guides our actions, not the other way around.

When I realize that it's my heart that drives my actions, it makes sense that I need to prioritize heart goals over performance goals. But what does it mean to have goals of the heart? Running a mile in under four minutes makes sense. It's easy to visualize and quantify. It's less easy to define a heart goal. While heart goals are less tangible than performance goals, they don't have to be nebulous. My approach to setting goals of the heart was to pick one heart condition I wanted to go after in each competition. A heart goal would be running the Boston Marathon out of a heart of courage, knowing that if I already have Jesus, there is nothing better to add to my life than what I already have. A goal like this enabled me to run free of failure and full of courage.

The list of heart conditions one could go after seems to be limitless: Peace. Loving others. Joy. Encouraging others. Trust. Contentment. Worshiping God. Patience. Self-control. I found that to achieve my heart goal, I needed to put it in the forefront of my mind, similar to how I used to put times or places I wanted to achieve in the forefront of my mind. A way to do this was to turn that goal into a declaration or mantra that I repeated as I ran. If my goal was to run with a heart of joy, I might tell myself, "Find joy in the suffering." It takes a lot of focus to achieve any goal, but especially to achieve a heart goal.

Having a heart goal always reassured me whenever I toed the starting line of a race. I didn't know how fast I was going to run or what place I was going to finish in, but I knew that I could accomplish my goal of running with a right heart. More important, I knew that if I ran with a right heart, the performance would be pleasing both to God and to me. I truly believed and experienced that running with a right heart allowed me to push harder and go deeper than I had before.

When I began to pursue heart goals instead of performance goals, I didn't stop setting physical goals for myself. Of course I was motivated to break an hour in the half marathon or run a marathon in 2:04, but those goals became more lighthearted and fun, almost like the icing on the cake. Achieving them was no longer the way I defined victory. They were simply enjoyable and motivating extras to go after, but I didn't have to achieve them to see myself as successful. Setting heart goals as my main goals liberated my physical goals and allowed me a greater chance to realize them.

There's a verse I reflected on often when I was in the process of changing my emphasis to heart-based goals. It's 2 Chronicles 16:9: "For the eyes of the LORD move to and fro throughout the earth that He may strongly support those whose heart is completely His." I want my heart to be completely His, because there is nothing better than being that intimate with God. In all things, I want to think about my heart more than I think about my performance. I truly believe it is the only goal that leaves me feeling light and free, knowing that I have the opportunity to accomplish my goal every time I toe the line.

Failure

I'll never forget a pastor saying one Sunday that if you are going to be a big dreamer, you had better develop equally big resilience. Those words really resonated with me because I'd always been a big dreamer, but I hadn't considered the cost that would come with it. In my running career, I'd had plenty of failures. The ones that stuck out the most were my costing my team an NCAA cross-country team championship during my freshman year at Stanford when we lost by one point—a point I would have easily scored if I had run close to my potential—and failing to qualify for the NCAA Track and Field Championships during my first three years at Stanford. If I had parallel lists of races I deemed successes and races I deemed failures, the failures list would probably be twice as long.

Only a month before the 2011 Boston Marathon, where I had one of my greatest successes and ran my fastest time ever (2:04:58), I'd suffered one of the biggest failures of my career. I had been training in the thin air of Flagstaff, Arizona (seven thousand feet), and was running some of the best workouts of my life. I'd routinely do fifteen-mile tempo runs near a five-minutes-per-mile pace on hilly courses. I was feeling strong and running times in workouts that I had never touched before, so I expected my races to be breakthroughs as well. I couldn't wait to go out and test my fitness against some of the world's best runners at the New York City Half Marathon as a tune-up a month before my goal marathon.

Many times in my career, I found that I fell the hardest when my expectations were the highest. Obviously, it's a positive thing to have your training going well when you have a major competition on the horizon, but usually if my high level of fitness led me to believe that the race would be easy, I was setting myself up for a big disappointment. I learned to arrive at the starting line of every race expecting it to be hard, to hurt worse than ever before, and to be an epic challenge. Generally when I had this mindset, I was surprised that the race wasn't as hard as I'd anticipated. But this wasn't my mindset prior to the 2011 New York City Half Marathon.

My expectation going into the NYC Half was that I could challenge my American record of 59:43. But once the gun fired and we were off, I could manage to run only the first couple of miles with the leaders at a humble pace (well slower than the 4:32 pace required to better my American record) before losing contact with the lead pack and fading a "long, slow death." (I coined this phrase after experiencing this so many times in my career.) I ended up finishing more than five minutes slower than my personal best, which for a world-class runner amounts to the difference between running with the best runners in the world and recreational jogging. I was devastated. The worst part was I didn't even have an excuse for my performance. I envied the runners who could blame their bad performance on what they had eaten the night before, illness, or injury. That usually wasn't my story. Often when I didn't perform well, the cause was a bit of a mystery to me, which I found maddening.

The NYC Half Marathon finished in Manhattan's Battery Park, about four miles away from the starting line in Central Park. After the race, I decided to "walk it off" to process what had just happened. I set off on the four-mile trek back to the start, stopping several times to grab coffee in the hope that the caffeine would lead my mind to some grand revelation explaining the dismal day—or at least put me in a better mood. The caffeine did make for a wired walk, but even it could not lift my broken spirit.

When I reflect on the many heartbreaks of my running career, I'm able to identify what helped me get through them: I had to keep moving forward. It has been said, "If you're going to fall, fall forward," which to me means that you need to learn from your mistakes. But there's more to it than that. Moving forward involves having a vision for your future that is bigger than the heartbreak you are going through. For me, walking the streets of Manhattan after the NYC Half Marathon and turning inward only made things worse. What helped me was getting up the next morning and thinking about Boston, which was only a month out. Thinking about Boston gave me hope. My training had been going phenomenally well, I was healthy, and everything—aside from the NYC Half— was clicking. I once heard on the radio that athletes need to develop amnesia about their poor performances, and I've found that to be true. Obviously, you want to learn from your mistakes, but you also want to be so focused on what is right in front of you that the past isn't in your mind at all—you've forgotten it.

God illustrates "sports amnesia" when He tells us, "I, even I, am the one who wipes out your transgressions for My own sake, and I will not remember your sins" (Isa. 43:25). How amazing is that! God doesn't even remember my sins, yet I continue to beat myself up over them for days, weeks, and sometimes months, which usually only causes me to struggle even more with sin. Later in the Bible, Paul affirms this attitude of forgetting the past and focusing on what is ahead when he says, "Brethren, I do not regard myself as having laid hold of it yet; but one thing I do: forgetting what lies behind and reaching forward to what lies ahead, I press on toward the goal for the prize of the upward call of God in Christ Jesus" (Phil. 3:13–14).

If we are to live out our destinies and accomplish greatness in our lives, we must realize that failure is a necessary part of the process and something we shouldn't try to avoid. Failure can teach us and make us stronger, but this doesn't mean that we should dwell on it. God was constantly telling the Israelites to make memorials to the Lord so they wouldn't forget what He had done for them. He never told them to think about all the times He didn't show up the way they wanted Him to. Their focus was to be on what God was doing, not on what they thought He didn't do. I say "what they thought He didn't do" because God never fails us. He doesn't always meet our expectations, because He is the only one who knows the big picture, so only He truly knows what is best for us. In tough times, we need to be reminded that God is the ultimate Father and will never fail us. He shows up exactly how we need Him to in every situation. We just need to take off the glasses of our expectations so we can see Him.

A month after my epic failure, I found myself on the starting line of the Boston Marathon with a smile on my face. Boston is a point-to-point (one way) course starting in Hopkinton and finishing in downtown Boston. I had run the race two times before and both times had battled pesky crosswinds and headwinds. Because I'm a natural frontrunner, wind is not my friend. Bill Rodgers (four-time winner of the Boston Marathon) had told me that once every ten years, runners get a wicked tailwind that pushes them all the way to the finish. This happened to be one of those years. I had never had the opportunity—and never would again—to run Boston at my level of training with a tailwind pushing me from start to finish.

What ensued was the fastest marathon ever run in history. I was at the front of the pack, leading a group of all African runners until the twenty-mile mark. When we came through the halfway point in under sixty-two minutes, the race director, Dave McGillivray, radioed from his motorcycle (which was following the leaders) to his timing team that the clocks on the course were messed up, because they were displaying a time in the sixty-ones. But they weren't. At the time, the world record in the marathon was just under 2:04, and everyone in that lead pack was on pace to break the world record. At mile twenty, the top two guys pulled away from me. I was in a world of pain, unable to respond to their surge, but that didn't dampen my spirits. Every time I looked at my watch and saw mile after mile clicking away at a 4:45 pace, I was filled with excitement, knowing that I was running this marathon far faster than I ever had run one before.

With just one mile to go, the clock on the course read two hours flat. I knew I was going to shatter my personal best (2:06:17 at the 2008 London Marathon) and the 115-year-old course record of 2:05:52, despite being in fourth position, with the third-place runner just steps in front of me. The question was, How fast would I run? After seeing the clock, I had a discussion with myself. I had never hurt this badly in a race, which caused me to consider two options. I could chill the last mile and run it in about 5:30 or so and enjoy myself. I'd still run 2:05 and change, which sounded good to me. Or I could put my head down and run a gut-wrenching final mile, enduring what would seem like an eternity of pain in an attempt to run under five minutes and thus under 2:05 for the marathon. As I considered my options, the thought came crashing into my head that I might never be in this position again—which turned out to be true—so I decided to take the pain-filled option. When I crossed the finishing line and saw the clock reading 2:04:58, I clapped my hands, feeling the same joy as if I had won the race. The winner, Geoffrey Mutai, and second-place runner, Moses Mosop, finished close to 2:03 flat, shattering the world record. But the Boston Marathon is not eligible for world or American records because it is a net downhill as well as point-to-point course, both of which are disqualifying features. None of that mattered to me, though. I had pushed myself harder than ever before and discovered what God had put inside me. I couldn't have been happier.

Looking at my Boston Marathon triumph in light of the failure I'd experienced one month before, I realized that the two moments were connected. One couldn't have happened without the other. For reasons outside of my understanding, after the NYC Half, it was like a switch had gone on in my legs and in that last month before Boston I was training at a much higher level. I still can't comprehend why I felt such a major jump in my physical fitness, but it was so apparent that I cannot deny that something about that heartbreaking race woke me up physically, mentally, emotionally, and spiritually. This experience helped me realize how intimately connected success and failure are, but the only way to reap the benefits of failure is to handle it properly. I never would have experienced the breakthrough in Boston if I'd lost hope and stopped moving forward after NYC.

Hope is what we're all looking for in our moments of failure, but it can be difficult to find, which makes it even more challenging to move forward. I find that talking to others can help me restore my vision as well as understand how failure is part of the journey toward victory. Another method of not only restoring but also maintaining hope is to see the failure coming. It's not so much that I expect to fail but rather that I know it is failure that will make me strong enough to succeed. Accepting that failure is part of the process is the only way to get where I want to go. Paul commands us to "exult" with tribulation (I like to substitute "failure" for "tribulation"), "knowing that [failure] brings about perseverance; and perseverance, proven character; and proven character, hope; and hope does not disappoint, because the love of God has been poured out within our hearts through the Holy Spirit who was given to us" (Rom. 5:3–5).

I like to look at failure as resistance training. Now that my hobby is weightlifting, I realize more than ever that the best way for me to get stronger is to fail. I always use a power rack when bench pressing—it has safeties so if you are unable to lift the weight, you can easily set it down on the safeties—so I can put more weight on the bar than I can bench, then lower it as slowly as possible before setting it on the safeties. At first, I fail every single set because I cannot push the weight off my chest. But after a month or so of failing over and over with the same amount of weight, a breakthrough happens and soon I'm benching the weight that had defeated me so many times before.

We can experience failure for years and years. I think

about Joseph in the Bible enduring imprisonment for years before realizing his God-given dream to help protect God's chosen people from the famine that was to come. Or I think of Moses fleeing Pharaoh, only to hang out in the desert for forty years before acting on his mission to lead Israel out of slavery. It may not seem like it, but if you fail, you are still on the path to your destiny. You can still realize your vision. You are in the same company as David, Peter, Paul, Samson, and many other heroes of the Bible. The greatest example I can think of is Jesus, who endured His greatest "failure" just days before His greatest victory. He may very well have known that His dying on the cross wasn't failure, but that was because He was so connected to God's plan for His life. He shared God's vision. Jesus understood that what the world saw as His greatest defeat would result in the greatest victory the world has ever known.

. Just imagine how distraught Jesus' disciples must have been as they witnessed their leader being nailed to a cross and crucified. To them—and to the rest of the world—Jesus' death was a great failure. Yet it led to the restoration of relationship between God and those who accept Jesus' blood as payment for all of their sins. We need to keep this in mind as we attempt to change the way we see failures in our lives. Rather than being discouraged by them, we need to see them as weights that are making us strong enough to succeed.

Positive Focus

My getting into running in the late nineties happened to coincide with the genesis of the internet and online chatrooms. One day at a friend's house, I entered an online chatroom for runners, expecting it to be fun and inspiring. I recall being surprised to see my name in a chat and being intrigued. But as I read some of the critical comments thrown around in anonymity, I no longer enjoyed reading them. The funny thing is that even though most of the comments were positive, it was those few negative words sprinkled in that stuck with me. In the weeks and months that followed, I thought about those negative remarks throughout the day, especially when I was doing a hard workout. I wanted to prove those commenters wrong, so I decided to use their comments as fuel for my fire. There was one problem, though. I never had my best workouts or races when I ran with someone's negative words floating around in my head, which makes sense, because I firmly believe that whatever you focus on will increase. If I focused on negative comments in workouts, I usually tried too hard because I was trying to prove myself. And trying too hard caused me to tighten up. Nothing good happens in running, or in most sports, when you get tight. Tight muscles never outperform loose muscles simply because their range of motion is restricted, meaning they can't move the full length for optimal power. Over my career, I had to learn to quiet the negative voices around me and focus on good things so I could run relaxed and fast.

Whatever we fix our minds on grows, which is why it's so important to monitor our thoughts. Perhaps this is why Paul tells Christians, "Whatever is true, whatever is honorable, whatever is right, whatever is pure, whatever is lovely, whatever is of good repute, if there is any excellence and if anything worthy of praise, dwell on these things" (Phil. 4:8). I find it interesting to note what is excluded from Paul's comments. He doesn't tell us to dwell on the criticisms of peers. He doesn't tell us to dwell on all the things that are going wrong in our lives. He doesn't encourage us to beat ourselves up over what we imagine others think of us. Reading Paul's words encourages me to pull my mind away from all the chatter and negativity around me and set my mind on good, true, and hope-filled things.

I usually had my best races and workouts when I was just having fun, enjoying the sensation of running and the pain that comes with pushing myself, focused on living out my God-given mission. On those runs, I wasn't focused on what others said I wasn't capable of. I was focused on what God had shown me was possible for my life. The more I was able to set my mind on what God said, rather than on what others say, the more confident I became and thus the better I ran. God's words are only positive, hopeful, and truthful, so setting my mind and heart on them caused positivity and strength to flow through my running and my life.

God speaks to me and into my situations in different

ways, but probably the way I lean on the most is reading His words in the Bible. I remember that in the nerve-wracking weeks prior to the 2003 NCAA Division 1 Cross-Country Championships—the most important race of the year for a collegiate runner, but the one I'd seemed unable to get right the previous two years—I was reading my Bible one morning and came across this passage: "He says, 'You are My war-club, My weapon of war'" (Jer. 51:20). Now, I understand that athletics is not the context of this passage, but what it conveys is that God can inhabit us with His Spirit for a powerful and profound purpose. It gave me the chills to think of God looking at me as someone He could use as a powerful tool to advance His kingdom as in a battle. It felt to me like the Holy Spirit was imparting into the deepest part of my heart the identity that I could be useful. A few weeks later while I was running in the NCAA Championships race, I remember repeating those words to myself: "I am His war-club, His weapon of war." I might not have been fighting an actual war that day, but there was a war inside my mind between the voice of the critics, saying, "You have run poorly at the NCAA Championships every year you've run," and the voice of God, declaring, "You are My war-club." Repeating the voice of God was the only way I knew to make the voice of the critics fade away. As a result, I had a breakthrough performance, leading most of the race and placing second at the national championships while leading my team to the title. That race is still one of the most precious memories of my career.

After I became aware of how the dwellings of my mind affected my performance, I stopped entering online chatrooms and reading internet message boards. I also stopped reading, listening to, or watching any media about myself. To this day, I still haven't read any articles about me during my professional career. It's not that I dislike the media attention or distrust the media. I see great value and influence in the media, and I find it intriguing and inspirational to read articles and listen to interviews about my favorite teams, athletes, and people. But I found that for my success, I had to prevent negativity and doubts from entering my mind so that I could be fueled by positivity and not hindered from performing at my highest level.

There may be a lot of critics out there, but my toughest critic has always been me. I too often beat myself up over bad races, missed opportunities, and poor choices. It took a lot of work to combat my own criticism and to extend grace to myself. Though I find it pretty easy to extend grace to others, I often struggle to forgive myself for my shortcomings. Once again, the key lies in looking at myself through God's eyes. My pastor, Bill Johnson, often says, "I can't afford to have a thought about myself that God doesn't have about me." God's grace has covered my failures, and now He looks at me with unconditional love, a love that doesn't have to be earned and can't be lost. If God, who Himself is perfect, can extend grace to me, then certainly I should be able to extend grace to myself. Running free of the criticism of others is one thing, but I also have to run free of my criticism of myself.

Another reason that, even at the height of my career, I didn't like to pay attention to media about me is because it could have caused me to think more highly of myself than I ought, as well as added pressure to perform to others' expectations. My most vivid memory of this happening was during my sophomore year in high school. It was my first time at the California State Cross-Country Championships, and I had been running well leading up to the race, so my expectations were already pretty high. Then, after jogging the course the day before my competition, I read the short blurb written in the program about my race and what others should expect. They mentioned my name, and then predicted who they thought was going to win. Surprise, followed by joy, then pressure coursed through my body as I read that I was the predicted winner. I can still vividly remember getting chills. *They think I'm going to win* kept repeating in my mind. My already heavy expectations for myself seemed to double. As you can imagine, the next day I was not running light and free but instead was weighed down by pressure. I ended up fourth, well below all my performances of the year and below my potential. At the time, I didn't think my negative performance was because of pressure, but now I can see that the external pressure pushed me over the edge and caused me to run tight and fearful of letting myself and others down.

Today, I've found that criticism isn't just in articles that I'd have to seek out but also in social media, where comments can be hard to avoid. Back in 2010, I endured a massive disappointment in having to withdraw from the Chicago Marathon and had to make the announcement on Twitter. It was a vulnerable post expressing my grief in that moment. I remember it was hard to resist scrolling through comments in response to my post. Ninety-nine percent of the comments were encouraging and well-wishing, but today—eight years later—I couldn't tell you what any of those positive comments said. But I do remember clearly the only negative comment. It stuck with me and made me doubt my abilities. That is how powerful negativity can be and illustrates why we have to avoid it.

I've come to realize that only one person's opinion of me matters—God's. Jesus states, "I do not receive glory from men. . . . How can you believe, when you receive glory from one another and you do not seek the glory that is from the one and only God?" (John 5:41, 44). I see receiving glory as the place from which we get our validation. Glory is determined by our worth, our sense of how special, loved, and valuable we are. I don't think Jesus is saying it's wrong to receive compliments or words of affirmation from people other than God—I believe that God often encourages us through the words of others. Yet there's a difference between receiving glory and receiving compliments and encouragement. By reading the words that were written about me in those chatrooms, I was inadvertently seeking glory from others. The glory of man is fickle and dependent on our performances, whereas the glory of God is rooted in His unshakable, undying, unrelenting love for us simply because He loves us for who we are, and that can never be shaken by our performances.

Even if I know that my glory comes from God, I still need to be careful whom I allow to speak into my life. Even if you can easily shake off a person's negative comments, I would still argue that it is better not to surround yourself with such people or even to view their comments. The wrong people can so easily distract us from our God-given mission. Jesus was guarded in His interactions with others: "From that time Jesus began to show His disciples that He must go to Jerusalem, and suffer many things from the elders and chief priests and scribes, and be killed, and be raised up on the third day. Peter took Him aside and began to rebuke Him, saying, 'God forbid it, Lord! This shall never happen to You.' But He turned and said to Peter, 'Get behind Me, Satan! You are a stumbling block to Me; for you are not setting your mind on God's interests, but man's'" (Matt. 16:21–23).

Jesus was good at quickly identifying stumbling blocks that would trip Him up as He set out to accomplish God's mission. Imagine that Jesus had been concerned with Peter's rebuke and had even let it influence how He lived out His last days. Fortunately, He refused to allow others' comments to derail Him or set Him back from fulfilling His mission. Like Jesus, we must be set on pleasing God and no one else. We can't become distracted by the comments of others, but we must keep our focus on His words about us and giving Him the glory.

When I am running with this focus, I can have joy whether I'm having the best workout of my life or the worst one ever, whether I'm winning a race or just struggling to finish. When the cheering crowds and the critics fade away, I can feel the smile on His face as He watches me compete. And as a dad of four girls, I get this. It doesn't matter what sport they're playing or how well they're doing, I just love to watch my girls compete. I love watching them go after maximizing their God-given potential. I can't help but think that if I take such delight in watching my kids compete, how much more delight must God take in watching His children compete. So let us focus on the delight of our Father as we walk securely and confidently, hopeful that we are bringing pleasure to the one who created us for that purpose.

Humility

On a pleasantly warm, blue-skied day in Mammoth Lakes, California, my fellow Mammoth Track Club teammate Ian Dobson and I were enjoying a nice easy run on meandering soft dirt roads that almost seemed to massage our tired legs back into form after a grueling session the previous day. Our conversation flowed from this to that, as it typically does on an easy run when you can let your mind wander. At some point, we talked about our running plans. We had just finished our collegiate running careers at Stanford, where we had focused on cross-country (10K) and had just finished one-two in the 5,000 meters at the 2005 NCAA Track and Field Championships. A week after that race, we finished two-three in the 5,000 at the USA National Championships, which gave us the opportunity to compete in the World Championships that summer. Worlds had not gone well for me. I had led early in my preliminary heat before fading badly, not even getting close to qualifying for the final. Now, back into training months later in the fall, we were looking ahead to the 2008 Beijing Olympics and trying to figure out which event each of us would be best suited to make a run at qualifying in.

To the outside observer—and perhaps even to our coach—it must have seemed obvious that our best bet would be the 5K or 10K on the track. We were young and had just qualified for the World Championships, and on the track is where the most talented runners competed. The conventional line of thinking was to stick to the track as long as you could—usually until you hit about thirty—and then move to the marathon and road racing in the twilight of your career. You would race a few marathons before conceding to Father Age and hanging up your racing shoes. The roads were seen by elite runners as more of an afterthought to their careers, a way to pick up some additional money rather than being a respectable goal.

This mentality was changing, though, as more and more young Kenyan and Ethiopian athletes dominated the roads. I had done a few road races, but my passion had always been the track. When I was getting into the sport, I remember watching the movie *Prefontaine* and really resonating with Pre's mentality of "I'm not going to let anyone tell me I'm not fast enough to run the mile." Like Steve Prefontaine, I was determined to be a miler even though my footspeed was lagging. (I could run 400 meters in fifty-one seconds, but to be a world-class miler, you really needed to have sub-fifty 400-meter speed.)

One would think that the fact that God had given me a vision for my first run to be fifteen miles would send a pretty clear signal that He was calling me to distance running. (The mile is considered middle distance.) Somehow, though, I missed that signal. I was determined to follow in the footsteps of my heroes, Jim Ryun (former world record holder for the mile) and Hicham El Guerrouj (current world record holder for the mile), and become one of the best milers in the world.

The problem was that after clocking 3:42 for 1,500 meters (equivalent to a 4:00 mile) as a senior in high school, I stopped improving, though not for a lack of ingenuity or effort. As a freshman in college, I wanted so badly to be a miler that I focused on the 800 meters in an attempt to gain the footspeed I was lacking. It makes me laugh now to look back at how I ran the 4 x 800 meters at the Penn Relays. I had no business being in that race, but my pride had kept me from competing in my true area of giftedness—long distance running. I continued to focus on the mile throughout my sophomore year and had another tough season, seeing no improvement despite a work ethic that drove me to run three times a day.

My junior year of college coincided with the 2004 Olympic Games in Athens, Greece. I knew it would take a miracle for me to get there, but that didn't keep me from dreaming. I had everything I needed—a great coach, the perfect place to train, fast and motivated teammates to train with, and all the support that comes with participating in division 1 athletics. My only problem was that I was training for the wrong event.

In collegiate cross-country, all the men's races are an 8K distance until you get to the regional and national championship races, which are both 10K—which seemed way farther than I wanted to run. Most milers are decent in cross-country, but they don't dominate the sport because of the sheer distance of the races. My first year at Stanford, our cross-country team ended up losing the national championship title to Colorado by just one point. I'm sure each guy blamed himself for not passing one more person, but I took the loss particularly hard because I'd been winning races early in the season but had tanked by NCAAs. If I had performed as well as I should have, Stanford would have won the title. That was hard to take.

My sophomore year, our team tasted redemption and won the NCAA title, but not thanks to my performance. Once again, I began the season in phenomenal shape but ended it running horribly. When I look back at those first two seasons of cross-country, it's easy for me to see that it was pride that was killing me. Instead of doing the prescribed summer training—which was way too easy, in my mind—I decided to make up my own training, focusing on high-intensity interval training rather than the foundational base training (a lot of running but at a lower intensity level) I should have been doing. I thought I knew better than my coach how to reach my goals, and this attitude was the root of a lot of the pride I battled throughout my career and continue to work on today. Often, pride boils down to a lack of trust. If I trust that God or my coach or whoever is in a position of authority over me knows better than I do, then I will do what they say. The only way I seemed to be able to learn this lesson was through heartbreak. My sophomore year of college, I finished the 10K at the NCAA Cross-Country Championships far behind my teammates and outside of the top thirty finishers. When my dad found me after the race, I was collapsed on the ground more from disappointment than from exhaustion. I remember telling him that I never wanted to run the 10K again. If only I could have fast-forwarded just one year and seen what was about to happen!

It took me two years to learn to trust my coach's summer workout plan, which was unfortunate, because his plan led runners to national titles. In the summer before my junior year, I set my mind to do exactly what my coach had prescribed over the summer. I put in all the foundational work that had been missing in previous years, and when I returned to school that fall, I wasn't in as good of shape as I'd been the previous two years, but I was in the *right* kind of shape. I had built a strong foundation, so when our coach had us engage in heavy interval training, my body was ready for it. As the season went on, I got better and better. And something else shifted as I learned to let go of my pride. I started to work with my teammates in training, rather than treating every practice as an opportunity to prove my fitness. Rather than trying to drop my teammates, I instead encouraged them and took my foot off the gas if I felt they started to fade. I was finally running my workouts how my coach had designed them: controlled and within myself.

As I mentioned, my junior year at the NCAA Cross-Country Championships remains one of the most cherished memories of my career because I led our team to another NCAA championship. I finished second overall, and our team scored the second lowest point total (twenty-four) in NCAA history. (In cross-country, the lowest point total wins.) I never would have had this experience had I not won the battle in my mind and also swallowed my pride and trusted my coach while learning how to run with my teammates.

The victories over my pride kept coming during the track season, despite the fact that I wasn't particularly successful that year. (I ended the season injured and unable to compete at the NCAA Championships.) For the first time, I opened up my heart and mind to the idea that God hadn't designed me to be a miler. I dabbled in longer races, and I discovered that when you're functioning within your giftedness, things click. Immediately, I started seeing far better results than I'd had when I was training for the mile. And as I functioned within my area of giftedness, I started to enjoy running more. When I was training like an 800/1,500 runner, I didn't particularly enjoy the training—or racing—because I felt like I was always beating my head against a wall, trying hard but not getting anywhere. With the longer distances, the races just seemed to flow out of me with less effort, and the sensation of running just felt better.

Today, I'm still going after many virtues I need to grow in, such as humility. And I'm continuing to realize that if I start with a little—maybe just one small step in the right direction—those virtues will grow. Discipline begets discipline. Self-control grows self-control. Patience results in more patience. And a little humility makes it easier to become even more humble. Small changes are so much easier to accomplish, and they add up to big changes in the long run.

During my run in the forest with Ian, I told him something along the lines of, "If I have to turn to the roads at a young age and focus on longer distances, I would do that if that's what I was best at." That comment might not seem profound, but it took me years and years of work to finally admit that I was going to follow the giftedness God had given me rather than just do what I wanted to do because of the prestige of competing on the track.

A beautiful thing happens when we let go of our pride and trust our creator. When we trust, we experience peace—the peace of not having to be in control, the peace of knowing that God is good and has good plans for us. I don't like to spend much time speculating about what my life might have been like had I allowed my pride to cause me to miss all that God had for me. But there likely would have been no Olympics, no American records, and I likely would have retired from the sport prematurely after battling the frustration of trying to become a world-class miler and getting nowhere.

I don't necessarily think that while I focused on shorter distance races, God caused all my struggles in order to wear down my pride. I see them more as a natural consequence of having pride in my heart. Because I wasn't listening to God's guidance, I wasn't doing what I was designed to do and thus was really struggling. I'm glad that eventually I let go of what I thought was best for me and started looking to God to guide my steps. It turns out He is much better at showing me the way than I am at determining it on my own. I learned that God may have given me a vision to run with the best guys in the world, but how I got there had to be determined by Him, not me. It would have been a tragic ending to my story had I remained stubborn and never transitioned to the roads and marathon. Perhaps this is why the Bible says, "Pride goes before destruction, a haughty spirit before a fall" (Prov. 16:18 NIV).

Relationships

"Hey, Sara, hold on for a second" were the words I heard as I was passing. I was a junior in high school and had just raced the 1,500 meters at the Mt. SAC Relays in Southern California. I'd gone out far too fast (fifty-nine seconds for my first 400 meters) and had died the dreaded slow death, finishing in second place in 3:55. I was making my way out of the stadium, which was packed with high school runners from all over the US, when I noticed this girl. I didn't know her, but I was struck by how beautiful she was, causing me to turn my head as I walked past.

I'd had a few girlfriends in middle school, but those "relationships" didn't really count. We mostly wrote letters back and forth and communicated via our friends. After about a week, the girl would usually get sick of my letters and send a friend to bring me the news that she no longer wanted to be my girlfriend. By the time I got to high school, I was so focused on my running that I never pursued any girls.

I didn't have a lot of interest in girls when I was in high school partially because I was so focused on my running but also because I was so tired from training that I didn't have the energy for anything else. Also, I was broke and didn't have my driver's license, plus my hormones were always low as a result of the high mileage I was doing. (Side note: if you're looking to tame your teenage boy's testosterone level, running is a great way to put a damper on it.) It took a lot to turn my head when a girl walked by, so when it did happen, it struck me as odd.

After this girl at Mt. SAC turned my head, I didn't ask her who she was or even say anything at all to her. I was shy and had little to no experience initiating a conversation with a member of the opposite sex. Also, I'd grown up as the middle child of five siblings, only one of which was a girl, so it was a lot easier for me to relate to guys than to girls. (It's funny for me to reflect on this now as a father of four girls.) Anyway, the moment nearly passed me by, but just when I was almost out of hearing distance, I heard someone say, "Sara, hold on a second." Bingo! I had a name.

On the two-hour drive back up the windy roads that led to Big Bear Lake, I put two and two together. I knew the girl who had told Sara to wait, because she was one of the best runners in the state. I'd also heard of this dominant female runner from Santa Rosa named Sara Bei, who was already one of the best runners in the country. I assumed that this was *the* Sara.

Fast-forward seven months to the California State Cross-Country Championships in Fresno. I had just won my second state title and was making my way out of the finishing chute when some younger runners came up to me and asked for my autograph. I signed my name for them along with my favorite Bible verse (Isa. 40:31). Later in the day, Sara won her fourth state title—the first high school girl in California to do so—and the same kids approached her with the same paper I'd signed for them. I'm amazed that Sara was actually able to read my scribbled autograph along with the Bible verse I had written down. She also signed her name and favorite Bible verse, and more important, she made the connection that I was also a Christian. Funny how the little things in life—like signing an autograph with a Bible verse—can lead to such significant alterations in the trajectory of our lives, like who we're going to marry.

A few days later, my mom came downstairs after checking the family email on the only computer we owned. She mentioned that I'd received an email from Sara Bei. Now, let me tell you that after that head-turning moment at Mt. SAC, I'd developed a little crush on Sara and had read a few articles about her. Plus, I'd heard a few things about her from my dad. He had told me about this girl who had been favored not only to qualify for the High School National Cross-Country Championships but also had a good chance of winning it. Unfortunately, she'd had a bad day and failed to qualify for Nationals at the Regional Championships. After having a good cry, she stuck around to congratulate the girls who had qualified, which showed her good heart toward her competitors. This caught my dad's attention, and he thought I could learn a thing or two about sportsmanship from this girl, because I wasn't spending any time clapping for my competitors after they'd beaten me.

Anyway, back to the email. My mom liked to "pull my chain" from time to time, and she had heard me talk about Sara and probably guessed that I had a little crush on her, so I one hundred percent assumed that she was having fun with me. I responded with something along the lines of, "Very funny, Mom." It took her a while to convince me that she was serious—I actually *did* have an email from Sara—and I tried to hide my excitement as I went to the computer to see what she had written.

I'll never forget her opening line: "Hi, my name is Sara Bei and I run for Montgomery High School." I almost started laughing because, to any high school runner in California, Sara Bei needed no introduction. But that was the humility with which she always conducted herself. Sara went on to say that she saw I had signed my autograph with a Bible verse and assumed I was a Christian, so she wanted to encourage me in my faith as well as in my running. After seeing my autograph, she had tracked down my parents' email from a mutual runner friend. We finally met in person the following week at the Footlocker Cross-Country Western Regional meet.

Western Regionals did not go well for me. The race was held at the historic Mt. SAC course, where I had raced three times a year for my entire high school career. I'd never lost a race on this course and had even broken a course record that was more than thirty years old. But on my very last race at Mt. SAC, Western Regionals, I finished fourth. I still qualified for Nationals, but I wasn't happy about the loss. Sara claims she saw me finish, rip my bib off my uniform, and kick it. (How's that for a first impression?) I still deny I actually did that—honestly, I can't remember doing it—but knowing myself and how poorly I handle defeat, if it didn't happen in the physical, it did happen in my heart.

Sara competed later in the day and had a solid race, easily qualifying for Nationals while making sure she hadn't pushed too hard. (She's always done a better job running with her head than I have.) She handled her loss pretty much the exact opposite of me, calm and collected and correctly reasoning that "it's only qualifying." To me, there was no such thing as qualifiers—there was only winning and losing. As you might imagine, I wasn't in the mood to meet a girl I wanted to make a good impression on, and honestly I didn't have the confidence or boldness to introduce myself to her. So it looked like our meeting wasn't going to happen.

Lucky for me, God had put Drew Ryun in my life. It's funny how just one person can have so much influence. Drew was this person for me. As I mentioned earlier, Jim Ryun was always a big hero of mine, and in my sophomore year, I learned of the camp the Ryuns put on every summer, Jim Ryun's Running Camp. (The camp is still going to this day, so if you are a high school runner or have a high school runner looking for a great summer experience, I highly recommend checking it out.) I decided to attend the camp the summer before my junior year, and it was there that I not only learned what it takes to be a great runner or to have great faith but also became part of the Ryun family. Don't get me wrong, I didn't marry into the family, but I was welcomed in by the Ryuns and treated like family.

Drew, one of Jim Ryun's sons, was at the tail end of his professional running career. I had told him about what an ideal setup we had training in Big Bear Lake, living at the same altitude as the runners in Kenya, yet being able to drive one hour down the mountain to train at sea level. There's a lot of science backing the live-high, train-low method of training, yet it's hard to find a place where you can do that without insanely long drives. Drew decided to come stay with us in Big Bear to pursue his running and also to work on a book he was writing with his dad and twin brother, Ned. I'm so thankful Drew was an integral part of that season in my life. He was the one who introduced me to Sara that day at Mt. SAC, and he was also the one who introduced me to the coach at Stanford despite the fact I didn't want to go to school there at that time. Both of these introductions and relationships changed my life. To this day, I'm still good friends with Drew and the Ryun family. That kind of relationship outlasts running careers.

I always loved how Drew approached others to introduce himself with so much confidence and swagger. It was usually the same line: "Hi, my name is Drew Ryun, Jim Ryun's son." What I loved is that he appeared supremely confident in himself, probably for a host of reasons, but to me it seemed like one main reason was because of who his dad was. I like to think about that when I'm not feeling confident in who I am. I like to remember that I can get the same confidence Drew got from being Jim Ryun's son by realizing that I am a child of God, and this reality changes everything about how important, influential, and worthy of talking to I am.

I don't remember many details of that initial conversation with Sara besides being super nervous. Our conversation was short and nothing significant was said, but it was nice to meet the person I'd heard so much about and had been emailing. We were very much on the same path of running, school, and faith. We spent a little more time together the following week at the Footlocker National Championships in Orlando, Florida, where I finished third behind the future American record holder in the 5K, Dathan Ritzenhein, and the future American record holder in the mile, Alan Webb. Sara had an upset victory with a thrilling sprint finish.

Our email exchanges continued throughout the indoor and outdoor track seasons during our senior year of high school, but because Sara lived in Northern California and I lived in Southern California, our paths didn't cross often. We were both taking recruiting trips to colleges and trying to figure out the next step in our lives. Sara decided pretty early on to attend

Stanford, and I joke that I waited to see where she was going before I chose my college, but that wasn't the case. On the first day of spring in my senior year, I found myself deep in prayer while sitting in a pew in the beautiful church in Stanford's main quad. I was slightly distracted by the blaring organ music, which sounded like it was from *The Phantom of the Opera*, filling the ornate church. I remember feeling deep in my spirit that God was bringing me to Stanford so that I could be a positive influence on the cross-country and track teams. After walking out of the church, I committed to Stanford, which meant that Sara and I were going to be teammates.

Sara and I spent more time together at the Stanford preseason cross-country camp in Mammoth Lakes, California. It seemed like every guy on the team had their eye on her too, so if I was going to pursue her, I had to move fast. Lucky for me, our freshman dorms were right next to each other, so we spent those first few weeks exploring campus together. It was during one of those early explorations that I finally worked up the nerve to ask Sara out to dinner at a sushi restaurant (even though I'd never had sushi before).

Our first date had many memorable—and, to be honest, kind of awkward—moments. I had no idea what I was doing, because this was the first real date I'd been on. It's a miracle I didn't screw it up. We covered many topics over dinner, including the fact that Sara had wanted to adopt kids ever since she was a young girl. This was the first time I'd ever met someone who wanted to adopt. I didn't have any negative associations with adoption—I'd just never been around adoptive parents or adoptees, so I didn't have a grid for it. That night was the first time adoption had entered my mind, and I really do believe that God started showing me His heart for adoption then.

At the end of the night, as we made our way back to the

dorms and were getting ready to say goodnight, I told her what a great time I'd had and that I would love to go out again sometime if she would. Simply yet firmly, Sara replied, "No." It was the longest, most uncomfortable second of my life before she followed it up with "I'm just joking. Of course I'd like to go out again." I had yet to understand her sarcastic sense of humor.

After that date, everything was pretty linear for us. We dated all four years of college without ever getting in a fight, got engaged a week after we graduated, and got married three months later. When I look back on the progression of our relationship, I can see how God used it in so many ways, one of which was to help me on my journey. College was hard for me. I never would have made it without Sara's love and support. During college, often she would be the only thing that was going well in my life. I joked that every winter quarter, I would be sick, injured, and having a severe outbreak of poison oak all at the same time. I needed someone to lift me through those challenges, and Sara was that person.

I share this story to say that there's no way I would have experienced the breakthroughs I did later in my career had I not had meaningful relationships, like my relationship with Sara. If we are to reach our God-given potential, it's going to happen through our relationships. I think that's how God designed life to be. He was the one who created Adam and then said it wasn't good that Adam was alone, so He designed community to help him and make him stronger (Gen. 2:18). When I think about why God made humans in the first place, it boils down to the fact that He created us so we could be in relationship with Him. Even apart from creation, God is in relationship with Himself (God, Jesus, and the Holy Spirit).

Not only do we need to view community as the way to

achieve our God-given potential, but also we must realize that loving relationships within community are what life is really all about. As Paul says, "If I speak with the tongues of men and of angels, but do not have love, I have become a noisy gong or a clanging cymbal. If I have the gift of prophecy, and know all mysteries and all knowledge; and if I have all faith, so as to remove mountains, but do not have love, I am nothing. And if I give all my possessions to feed the poor, and if I surrender my body to be burned, but do not have love, it profits me nothing" (1 Cor. 13:1–3).

If our reaching our fullest potential is not motivated by loving others, we miss what is truly important in life—loving God and loving others. Throughout my career, I often had blinders on because I was so focused on my running. And while I'm not saying that we must stop and befriend everyone we meet, we do need to take the focus off ourselves on occasion. Look at Jesus. He was able to minister to thousands, but He intimately invested in only twelve. Yet through those twelve friendships, He changed the world. That's why we need to look at our relationships and not our accomplishments as our true legacy. Considering how reaching our God-given potential can be motivated by love will change the way we go about our lives, including the manner in which we try to accomplish our goals.

Above all of my athletic accomplishments, I most value the people I've met and have built relationships with on my journey. If it weren't for running, I never would have met my wife, our four adopted daughters, or the amazing people at Stanford and the Mammoth Track Club, nor would I have made all of the amazing friends I now have around the world. As we develop a deeper sense of what is truly valuable in this life, we must focus on the relationships we build. After all, the purpose of reaching our full potential in any endeavor is to better others. We can't be so self-focused that we miss out on the relationships that God intended for us to both invest in and reap from.

I've spent a lot of time thinking and praying about how to become great at what I do, and I've felt that God answers me over and over that greatness comes in the context of and through community. His answer should come as no surprise to me, because I've certainly experienced this to be true in my running career. If it had not been for the support of Sara, along with family, friends, teammates, coaches, chiropractors, nutritionists, sports scientists, and many others, I would not have been able to reach the level of success I attained. But it's also important to remember that the people around us aren't just there to support us and serve us; we are also there to support them and serve them. The first couple of years I was retired from professional running, one of the most life-giving activities I did is run a free running program called the Redding Distance Project, a gap program that encouraged kids of all levels to train year round. The program ran during the winter months when schools don't offer track or cross-country. Going to practice and working with those kids filled me up in the same way that hitting a big workout used to fill me up. I'm convinced that serving others, especially when you're doing it in your area of giftedness, is one of the most gratifying and satisfying things you can do in life. What Jesus said is absolutely true: "It is more blessed to give than to receive" (Acts 20:35).

MILE 9

Identity

It was the winter quarter of my sophomore year, and everything was falling apart. I was running terribly, and I felt like my dream of running with the best guys in the world was slowly swirling down the toilet. I vividly remember waking up one morning, looking in the mirror, and not liking what I saw—a failure. I don't know if you can relate, but this has to be the worst way to start your day, and it can be a dark place to try to get yourself out of.

I decided that the best way to change myself was by changing my location. I mistakenly thought that if I could just go home—which was the last place where my running had been clicking—I would start training well again and would gain a more positive perspective of myself. I made the tough decision to leave Stanford unsure if I was going to return, which still pains me to think of. Because I went home expecting things to get immediately better, I was let down when my reflection in the mirror at home showed me the same guy I'd seen in the mirror at Stanford. My running didn't change for the better, and my depression grew worse. I remember lying in bed all day feeling like I had absolutely no reason to get up.

On days when I attempted to go for a run, I would jog about half a mile and then walk home—not because I was physically tired but because I was so broken up on the inside.

A turning point finally arrived, though. I was on a trip to the food bank with my pastor, and he asked me, "What's the last thing you knew, beyond a shadow of a doubt, that God called you to do?" My mind flitted back to the day I had sat in the beautiful Stanford Memorial Church and asked God for wisdom about where I should go to college. In that moment, I felt strongly that God was telling me I should go to Stanford and start a Bible study with my new team. As I snapped back to reality at the food bank, I realized I had to return to Stanford, because I hadn't finished what God had sent me there to do.

Things didn't instantly change running-wise when I returned to Stanford, however. What did change, though, was my intentionality with God. Prior to my quarter off, I had been in the habit of doing personal Bible study and prayer times, but I would easily get distracted by the many demands facing college students. But when I returned to Stanford, I started regularly riding my bike to the massive football stadium on campus to read my Bible and to journal. Something about big stadiums has always captured me. I'm not sure what it is, but any time I'm in one I feel a sense of purpose and excitement. My time with God in Stanford Stadium was never long—maybe only thirty minutes—but it was focused, uninterrupted time in an environment in which it was easy for me to connect with God. I would dig into the Word and scribble down things I felt that God was telling me, and I always left the stadium feeling encouraged and better about myself and life.

My time with God was going the best it had ever gone, but I was still trying to juggle the complexities of being a Stanford student-athlete. I'd never had to manage my schedule before, trying to make time to read and study for my classes, go to my daily two- to three-hour practices, and then attend Bible studies and be involved in Christian groups on campus, like Athletes in Action. What was gradually changing, though, was the way I saw myself. I often fell into the trap of thinking that if I could change some behavior or perform at a higher level, I would like myself more. But this is a backward way to develop self-worth. I had to change the way I saw myself by realizing how God sees me.

During those times in the stadium, God showed me how He viewed me apart from my running. I came to understand that how I ran on the track had nothing to do with how God saw me. I already knew this in my head, but receiving direct communication from God made it truly hit my heart. Once I felt better about myself and what made me important apart from running, it wasn't as if the storms of my life quieted—they just didn't bother me as much anymore. In the spring, I ended my track season having gone another year without improving my high school mile time. I was bummed after my last race of the season, but my failure didn't rattle me as it once did, and that changed attitude enabled me to experience one of the biggest breakthroughs of my career the following fall in cross-country.

I love to read God's responses to Job and to Moses when they came to Him with their biggest problems. He responded with statements of "I am." Check out the story of Moses' crisis of identity when God tells him He wants to use him to free His people from Egypt:

> "Therefore, come now, and I will send you to Pharaoh, so that you may bring My people, the sons of Israel, out of

Egypt." But Moses said to God, "Who am I, that I should go to Pharaoh, and that I should bring the sons of Israel out of Egypt?" And He said, "Certainly I will be with you, and this shall be the sign to you that it is I who have sent you: when you have brought the people out of Egypt, you shall worship God at this mountain." Then Moses said to God, "Behold, I am going to the sons of Israel, and I will say to them, 'The God of your fathers has sent me to you.' Now they may say to me, 'What is His name?' What shall I say to them?" God said to Moses, "I AM WHO I AM"; and He said, "Thus you shall say to the sons of Israel, 'I AM has sent me to you.'" God, furthermore, said to Moses, "Thus you shall say to the sons of Israel, 'The LORD, the God of your fathers, the God of Abraham, the God of Isaac, and the God of Jacob, has sent me to you.' This is My name forever, and this is My memorial-name to all generations."

—EXODUS 3:10–15

I love how this exchange goes. God shows Moses a miracle—the burning bush—to kick things off, then the creator of the universe begins speaking with Moses. Think about that. You would think that if you heard God audibly, it would be pretty straightforward to trust Him and do what He tells you to do. Not only that, but God also tells Moses exactly what is going to happen. If you knew the positive result before you embarked on the journey, that would make it easy, right? But these things—the audible voice *and* knowing the result—aren't enough for Moses to go to Pharaoh. Moses' excuse? "I have never been eloquent in speech." Despite the miracles, the clear communication with God, and the prophecy, Moses is still caught up in his inadequacy. It seems crazy to me that Moses would have this struggle after this extraordinary interaction with God, yet I still feel that I can relate to Moses' feelings.

Even though I can hear from God, get a sign from God, and even receive a word of prophecy, I can still doubt myself. The question is this: Why do I doubt myself despite all God has told me and shown me? God addresses Moses' feelings of inadequacy by asking him questions that make him remember who God is. Questions like, "Who has made man's mouth?" While I would like to say that Moses is able to overcome his feelings of doubt and inadequacy once he has this revelation of who God is, he isn't. Instead, he requests that God send someone else. It's interesting to me that God doesn't become upset with Moses until after Moses—despite knowing exactly who God is and what He is capable of—refuses to go. Yet Moses is still so focused on his shortcomings that he isn't able to trust God's power and ability to work through him. Even so, God's redemptive plan can't be stopped. God appoints Aaron to go and speak on Moses' behalf.

Even if we don't have a proper view of our identity in Christ, God can still use us to accomplish His redemptive plan. But I think that Moses missed out on God's highest plan for him. I'm not sure what would have happened had Moses realized who God is—and therefore who he, Moses, was—but I have a feeling it would have been an even more incredible experience for Moses personally.

I still battle thoughts of inadequacy or even failure from time to time, but having experienced the heartbreak of dropping out of college for a while and seeing my hopes and dreams fade away, I've learned that often my biggest problem isn't what is happening in my life. Rather, it is how I see myself. I believe that the only way to know who we are is first to know who God is. When God reveals Himself to you and you understand that you are His child, made in His image, you can't help but feel adequate, powerful, and capable. When I'm going through tough times, I hear God telling me over and over, "Remember who you are." I've learned to develop "I am" statements that help me meet the challenges of life. When I feel tired in a race, I tell myself, "I am a warrior," or, "I am a champion," or, "I am victorious," or, "I am strong." These statements are all true, because God created me in His image and He is all of those things, but I've found that they don't always become a reality unless I declare them to myself. Perhaps this is why we are commanded to put on the belt of truth as part of our weapons of warfare (Eph. 6:14). If we don't remember the truth of who God is and who we are in Him, our armor is prone to slide off.

I began coaching high school cross-country in the fall of 2017, which was an amazing experience for me in so many different ways. I'm still learning the ropes of how to be a great coach, but I'm lucky to have had great coaching modeled for me throughout my career. I'm learning that as important as it is to design the proper workouts, make sure athletes do the training, and do all the little things right—stretching, nutrition, hydration—perhaps the most performance-enhancing thing I can do for my kids is to elevate how they see themselves. It is so clear to me that we run and perform and live out of what we believe about ourselves. This can be really great news, because I know that while a lot of my athletes just don't believe in themselves yet, they can always change their beliefs. Believing in yourself is a choice that becomes a practice. We aren't born believing in ourselves or not believing in ourselves; it's more that we have trained what we believe about ourselves by the thoughts we dwell on.

Think about an athlete who starts to have success in their

sport. What happens to their thought life? They start thinking more confidently. Maybe they start telling themselves, "I am really good at this." This thought gives them even more confidence, so they perform even better, maybe even reaching the point where they think, "I could be world class at this." And that thought leads them to holding and conducting themselves and practicing as a world-class athlete does.

Success breeds success. But what happens if you don't experience a success that starts the string of positive thoughts and belief in yourself? You still have to tell yourself the thoughts that successful athletes tell themselves before you can experience their success. Once you start believing you are world class, you will start acting like you are world class. This is why I work so hard to instill vision in my athletes. If they believe they can be great, they will expect to be great. They will have the goal of being great, and they will work toward that goal. They will train to become great. They will do all the little things that greatness requires. But it starts with positive thoughts and believing in who they are and what they can do.

I was lucky that God got ahold of me when I was thirteen and told me I would one day run with the best runners in the world. I embraced that vision of who I would one day become. I was never surprised by my success. I wasn't shocked that I made two Olympic teams or that I set American records. I knew the end before I got there. I had the vision.

Even if you haven't yet clearly seen the vision God has given you, you can still cultivate it and build it through your thoughts. You might start by asking, "What is true about me?" Better yet, ask, "What is true about who God is, and what does the answer to that question show me—who has been made in His image and likeness—about who I am?" When you build a positive thought life rooted in who God is and who He has created you to be, you will find life to be similar to how it was for me at Stanford when I returned after a quarter off. Your circumstances might not change right away, but they will affect you less. Your sense of value will be rooted no longer in how you perform but rather in who you are, which will free you from failure, secure in your unshakable identity.

Belief

When I was thirteen and just getting started in running, I overheard my dad telling someone he was worried I would run so hard that I would hurt myself. While this might just seem like the comment of a concerned dad, his statement was a seed of self-confidence that grew until I too believed I could push myself beyond my body's pain threshold. Having your father say he thinks you're that tough is extremely empowering. From that moment on, I always believed that I was mentally tough, and so I acted as a mentally tough runner would act when I ran. I'm sure I wasn't always as tough as I could have been in every workout or race, but believing that I was tough definitely made me mentally stronger.

The way to become a mentally tough runner is to believe you *are* a mentally tough runner. I know it's a little bit of circular logic, but it really is true. I realize that not everyone is blessed to have a father—or someone else in their life—who plants statements that blossom into strong beliefs. In that case, we need to be the ones who declare over ourselves, "I am mentally tough!" I find that declarations like this are especially powerful in moments of weakness, yet those moments are usually when we least feel like telling ourselves positive statements. It's much easier to partner with the negative and agree with thoughts like "I can't push myself any harder" and "This is so hard for me" and even "What's wrong with me?" We have to train ourselves for those battleground moments, and we must be prepared to declare what is true. And here's what is true:

- "For who has known the mind of the LORD, that he will instruct Him? But we have the mind of Christ" (1 Cor. 2:16).
- "But in all these things we overwhelmingly conquer through Him who loved us" (Rom. 8:37).

When I was running competitively and experienced self-doubt, I didn't always embrace the reality that I have the mind of Christ and that I overwhelmingly conquer through Him. It's hard to always have that mindset, and that's why we must train our thoughts so those truths are our reactions to impossible or overwhelming situations. I remember that whenever I lost contact with the leaders in a marathon, there was always a moment of panic, a sense that I was doomed, that my race was over and it was just going to get worse from here. Then I had to really battle and think the thoughts I wanted to think rather than the thoughts running through my mind. What helped me most was to take a deep breath, shake out my arms, then start feeding myself positive thoughts, ideally in the form of declarations.

I encourage you to prepare simple declarations to counter the negative thoughts that go through your mind when things get tough. The next time you're going through something hard, become aware of what you're thinking and flip those negative thoughts to the opposite. If you tend to tell yourself, "I'm just not very good at this," simply say to yourself, "I am working to become strong at this." You don't have to lie and pretend you are good at something that you are not, but you can flip that thought into a true and encouraging statement that will ignite hope in your spirit. You might not feel great in that moment of struggle, but the more you repeat that positive declaration in your head, the better you will feel about yourself and your ability to do what you imagine to be impossible. As 2 Corinthians 10:5 says, "We are destroying speculations and every lofty thing raised up against the knowledge of God, and we are taking every thought captive to the obedience of Christ." Taking thoughts captive is such a powerful practice because nearly every thought we have builds on another, so we must first become aware of the foundational thoughts we tell ourselves and address them.

Now that I coach other athletes, I often find that runners who start worrying about or questioning their mental abilities create wildfires of self-doubt that, if not reversed, can leave them powerless and in a really bad spot mentally. The worst thing that I can do is to agree that they are mentally weak or to question their mental capabilities, even if they have folded mentally. My job is to put out the fire of self-doubt and declare what is true about that runner and guide them to a place where they can speak powerful truths over themselves. If you have the opportunity to encourage those you train with or interact with, you can plant the seeds that grow into true grit. My belief that I was mentally tough started with someone else—my dad—first declaring that about me. Mental toughness isn't something you either have or don't have. Mental toughness starts with the belief that you are mentally tough, and it is nurtured through positive declarations.

I'll close this chapter with a verse that led me to victory in a half marathon in Philadelphia. I was at mile eleven, running in the lead group of Kenyan runners. We were all in a tremendous amount of pain, as was evident by our heavy breathing, the sweat pouring down our necks, and the grimaces on our faces. In this moment of intense suffering, a verse popped into my mind: "For as he thinks within himself, so he is" (Prov. 23:7). It was at this key moment in the race that I remembered that I will live out what I am thinking. If I believe I am tired, then I will notice how tired I am. If I believe I will surge at mile twelve, then I will be able to muster the strength I need because I believe that strength is there, and I will be empowered to search deep within my body to find it. After this realization, I told myself that I would surge hard at mile twelve, despite the intense pain I was feeling and despite the fact that surging felt like the last thing in the world I wanted to do. Because I was able to take that positive thought—that I could summon the energy to surge—and build it into a belief simply by repeating it in my head, I was able to dig into a place that I never would have accessed and pick up the pace dramatically. I ran my last mile in less than 4:30 to win the race. That victory will forever remind me of the power of my thoughts.

We need to believe the best about ourselves, focusing on what we want to increase in our bodies and in our lives. I got the idea that the way to become a mentally strong runner is to believe that I *am* a mentally strong runner from one of my pastors, Carl Richardson, when I asked him how I could know whether what I was hearing had actually come from God. Often I question what I think I'm hearing from God to the point that I no longer believe it's God speaking. Then weeks, months, or years later, I realize it *was* God who was speaking to me. This isn't to say that we shouldn't ever evaluate what we believe to be God's voice. We do need to practice discernment, but we also must believe that God wants to communicate with us and is speaking to us. We must believe we do hear from God. Probably the question I get the most from other runners is how to be mentally tough. You already *are* mentally tough. Maybe you just need to stop doubting or questioning your mental abilities. Believe that you are mentally tough and that foundational belief will lead to positive thoughts, which will lead to actions that show that you are mentally tough.

Success

I never would have made it to the level in running that I did had it not been for the practice of building monuments around my successes, meaning I used my successes, which at times were few and far between, to propel me through the valleys that lay between. Often I have pondered my four tough years at Stanford. Pretty much the only major successes I had there were at the 2003 Cross-Country Championships my junior year and then again in 2005, which was my senior year of track and field, when I won the NCAA division 1 national title in the 5,000 meters. That last track season was the only time in my four years at Stanford that I even qualified for the National Championships. My collegiate career, as well as my entire running career, endured because of a few glimpses of hope, glimpses that I felt God gave me to encourage me to keep going and pursue my vision and my dream of one day running with the best runners in the world. I felt that God was clearly instructing me to build "monuments" around these glimpses of hope much in the same way He instructed Israel in the Old Testament to build monuments (a pile of rocks, in this case) at places where God did remarkable things for Israel.

Joshua chapter 4 tells the story of how God commanded Joshua to take twelve stones from the dry land of the Jordan River, where He had parted the waters so that the Israelites could safely cross, and to use them to build a memorial or monument to God on the other side of the Jordan.

> Now when all the nation had finished crossing the Jordan, the LORD spoke to Joshua, saying, "Take for yourselves twelve men from the people, one man from each tribe, and command them, saying, 'Take up for yourselves twelve stones from here out of the middle of the Jordan, from the place where the priests' feet are standing firm, and carry them over with you and lay them down in the lodging place where you will lodge tonight.'" So Joshua called the twelve men whom he had appointed from the sons of Israel, one man from each tribe; and Joshua said to them, "Cross again to the ark of the LORD your God into the middle of the Jordan, and each of you take up a stone on his shoulder, according to the number of the tribes of the sons of Israel. Let this be a sign among you, so that when your children ask later, saying, 'What do these stones mean to you?' then you shall say to them, 'Because the waters of the Jordan were cut off before the ark of the covenant of the LORD; when it crossed the Jordan, the waters of the Jordan were cut off.' So these stones shall become a memorial to the sons of Israel forever."
>
> —JOSHUA 4:1–7

Something significant needed to be done so that Israel wouldn't forget the miracle God performed, something not only for that generation but also for generations to come. I don't know about you, but I forget the times God has shown up in my life unless I mark them by writing about them, telling someone else about them, or keeping some sort of record of them. This is what I mean by monuments—ways of remembering the times God has shown up in our lives.

When I was going through the wringer at Stanford, I was constantly reflecting on how God had shown up in my running, by looking at videos of races or simply by closing my eyes and remembering what it was like when I experienced His presence. As I focused on the positive things He had done and remembered the vision He had given me for my future, I was able to muster the strength to pick myself up off the ground and continue to put myself out there.

The opposite of building a monument to God is building a case against God. At times, frustration led me to focus not on what God was doing but rather on what God wasn't doing that I expected Him to be doing. It can be very easy for me to build a case against God, and when I do that, my relationship with Him isn't very healthy. After the 2012 Olympics, I had to deal with my shattered expectations of how I wanted God to show up. Going into the Games, I had recently set out on a journey to have "God as my coach" (more on that in a later chapter), which brought some high internal and external expectations of my results at the Games. Those were shattered when I dropped out of the race (which was the first time I had ever dropped out of any race). I was forced to deal with the disappointment and frustration of believing that God hadn't shown up in my running. When I focus on how God doesn't show up, I can build up so much offense toward Him that I stop praying and also stop believing that He will ever show up again, and this leads me down the dark road of disillusionment. Think about what happens when you are mad, disappointed, or frustrated with someone. Usually your anger results in a broken relationship in which communication is shut down and you avoid the person. Obviously this is not an ideal relationship to have with anyone, let alone with God. I've learned what works for me when I find myself going down this road. The first thing is to remember that I am not God. I am not all-knowing. I don't know what is best for me— only God knows that. As the Bible says, "'For My thoughts are not your thoughts, nor are your ways My ways,' declares the LORD. 'For as the heavens are higher than the earth, so are My ways higher than your ways and My thoughts than your thoughts'" (Isa. 55:8–9).

The next step in dealing with my offense toward God is to realize that He is the ultimate Father. Jesus, who knows God best, said, "If you then, being evil, know how to give good gifts to your children, how much more will your Father who is in heaven give what is good to those who ask Him!" (Matt. 7:11). When I relate to God as the best Father who has ever been or ever will be, it's easy for me to trust Him and believe that He knows what is best for me. Sometimes I just need to realign my definition of good with God's definition and trust that He knows what is good for me.

After I became a father three and a half years ago, a lot of what I knew about God the Father changed from head knowledge to understanding how God must feel about us as His adopted children. I know that I want the very best thing for my girls and would give anything for them to experience life to the fullest, but I also realize that some of the things they wish for will lead only to temporary happiness and cause emptiness in the long term. Candy makes an easy illustration of this point. I would love to let my kids experience the glory of eating sugary treats whenever they want, but I know that for their long-term health, this would not be a good parenting

strategy. (With that said, my daughter Jasmine and I are working on a kids' book titled *Candy Is Good for You*—stay tuned
for that one, because there actually is a time when candy is
good for you.) So I have to say no to my children sometimes.
But I also look for excuses to say yes as often as I can, so long
as what they're asking for isn't going to cause them pain and
make life harder for them. I feel that God also loves saying
yes to His children, even if this isn't always His response. I
can sometimes look back and see how His no was good for
me, but often I can't see the reason and am confronted with
the mystery of why. I've reached a point in my faith, though,
where I'm comfortable not knowing all the answers. I realize that I may never understand why God sometimes says
yes and at other times says no. Being okay with that mystery
comes down to trusting that God is the ultimate Father and
will always do what is best for His children.

I also have experienced joy when my kids are grateful for
the things I've either given them or done for them. Their gratitude fills my heart with joy, and when I feel appreciated, I
want to do even more for them. How much joy must it bring
to God the Father when we are thankful for the things He
has given us and the things He has done? Monuments are just
that—reminders that we should be thankful for what God
has done in our lives.

One of the best ways to show our appreciation for all He
has done for us is to share stories of how He has shown up
in our lives. I think of how good it makes me feel to hear my
kids tell their friends about something I have done for them.
It pulls on my heart and makes me want to do more. These
stories of faith not only reveal our gratitude to the Father but
also empower everyone who hears them by building up their
faith. Revelation 12:11 says, "And they overcame him because

of the blood of the Lamb and because of the word of their testimony." From this passage we can see that having monuments, or remembering how God has shown up in our lives, isn't only for propelling us along our journey. It's also meant to be a catalyst for other people to overcome their struggles. I see the power of testimony prominently displayed in sports, especially in team situations. I think about how hearing Meb Keflezighi and Deena Kastor talk about their breakthroughs in marathoning inspired me to experience my own breakthroughs.

If you are facing a challenge, remember that it is our ability to remember what God has done for us that allows us to conquer. I remember feeling shattered after injuries, poor workouts or races, or failed dreams and how if I shifted my focus away from those experiences and instead recalled strong races, solid workouts, and some of the amazing experiences I'd already had, my spirit lifted and I was filled with hope again. I've found that hope is the best fuel for my journey. Without hope, I wouldn't have any motivation to train or to do the hard work necessary to accomplish my mission, but with hope, I can endure the rocky—and at times treacherous—road to victory.

Maybe you don't feel like you have any monuments to build to God. If this is the case, I encourage you to take anything good that has happened in your life and use it as a monument. The best example I can think of in my day-to-day life is praying before meals. It's a way to pause to remember how grateful I am that God has provided me food to eat. There are so many little things for me to be thankful for. I can turn them into monuments because God has shown up as a good Father to give me these "little things." James 1:17 says, "Every good thing given and perfect gift is from above, coming down from the Father of lights, with whom there is no variation or shifting shadow."

My favorite tradition after the best races of my career was to save the shoes and singlet I raced in. I wouldn't even untie my shoes or wash my singlet after the race, because I wanted to preserve them in as close to race condition as I could. When I got back from those races, I would "retire" the jersey and shoes in my closet. Every time I got dressed in the morning, I'd see my singlets and shoes as monuments to what God had done, which was the most encouraging way for me to begin my day and feel ready for the trials that might come.

Comparison

I find it somewhat ironic when I share one of the biggest lessons God taught me: stop competing. I laugh because I competed as a runner for twenty years and was even paid for ten of them, which meant that compared with a lot of other people, I was fast. Even as a kid, I competed in baseball, football, and basketball, and a common adjective attached to my name was *competitive*, so it feels odd that the message to stop competing would come from me.

Let me clarify, though. When I felt that God was leading me to stop competing, I didn't feel He was addressing an outward action—such as not racing again—but rather I felt He was addressing what was happening in my mind and in my heart as I competed. Until that point, I was driven to be better than everyone else. My grid for success was comparison. How did I stack up with the rest of the field? This is a common but wrong mindset, and it caused me a lot of pain throughout my athletic career. I found that competing to be better than others was deeply unfulfilling and even a performance "de-enhancer." When I was competing to beat others, I put so much pressure on myself that if I failed, it shattered me. Perhaps part of that, for me, was being the middle of five children, a position that has made me always seek to stand out. One thing is for sure, though. Whether or not you are a middle child, most of us can relate to how good it feels to beat someone in something, whether it be a board game with the family or a race. Winning can be fun, but it can also be rooted in poisonous comparison.

I had a problem with comparison because I had an identity issue. I sought to beat others so I would feel valuable. Of course, that wasn't obvious to me at the time. I wasn't at bat thinking, *I'm going to hit a home run off you so I can feel special.* But I can see that it affected how I felt about myself. I know this was the case because I wasn't able to celebrate others' victories. I remember when I was a senior in high school with the goal of running a 3:55 mile and watching Alan Webb (funny to reflect on this, since Alan and I are friends now), who was also a senior in high school, run a 3:53 mile at the Prefontaine Classic. Watching him run that fast should have inspired me to think, *Hey, his breakthrough can be my breakthrough!* Instead, it had the opposite effect. I remember going to church shortly after watching the race and playing a game of pickup basketball after the service. I played very, shall we say, aggressively and even ended up in a scuffle with another kid. Alan's performance had made me feel worse about myself because I wrongly thought that when his stock value increased, my stock value decreased. I felt like I had lost worth. This is the comparison trap. It took me years and years of competing before I finally figured out that I don't have to compete in a way that is rooted in comparison.

Going back in my story to the time I spent with God in the empty Stanford football stadium, I felt He was encouraging me to think about my motives for competing. He kept highlighting the story of John and Peter in the gospel of John. In this story, the resurrected Jesus has just told Peter how he will die. Peter, with a heart rooted in comparison, responds by asking Jesus how John is going to die: "Peter, turning around, saw the disciple whom Jesus loved following them; the one who also had leaned back on His bosom at the supper and said, 'Lord, who is the one who betrays You?' So Peter seeing him said to Jesus, 'Lord, and what about this man?' Jesus said to him, 'If I want him to remain until I come, what is that to you? You follow Me!' Therefore this saying went out among the brethren that that disciple would not die; yet Jesus did not say to him that he would not die, but only, 'If I want him to remain until I come, what is that to you?'" (John 21:20–23).

I love how Jesus responds to Peter's comparing himself with John: "You follow Me." That's the same response I felt God giving me whenever I compared myself with others. He reminded me that my eyes were focused on something other than Jesus. When I compared myself with the best runners in the US, God responded, "You follow Me." When I was frustrated that I didn't make the podium after a race: "You follow Me." When I was upset that my workout hadn't been as good as someone else's: "You follow Me." Even when I compared myself with my previous performances: "You follow Me."

In athletics we tend to see ourselves in light of how we stack up with everyone else, but when we choose this view, we miss out on the beauty of how Jesus intends for us to compete. I can't think of anything good about comparing ourselves with others, but if we focus on Jesus and our journey, and are thankful for what God is doing and has done in our lives, then good things almost always happen. Even more than that, we feel a sense of fulfillment as we travel our path.

There are two types of marathons. The first type, paced

races, have a designated number of runners whose job is to set a fast pace for the first one-half to two-thirds of the race, allowing the other runners to tuck in behind them. (Running behind someone is a little easier than running alongside of or in front of someone, because there's less wind resistance.) When world records are set, it's always in paced races. There are also championship-style marathons—like the Olympic Marathon and the Boston Marathon, to name a few—where there is no pacesetter, so the pace is determined by the athletes. These races are usually won in slower times, since most runners don't like to run out front and break the wind for others, giving those who are running behind them an advantage. I, however, found that I ran my best at the front of the pack, breaking the wind and setting a fast pace regardless of whether the race was paced. I loved running at the front because I saw my athletic goal (how I wanted to compete) as a way to maximize my full potential (how fast I could run). I wasn't interested in running a slow, tactical race and defining my success by whether I beat everyone else. My goal was to get the most out of myself—as well as out of everyone else in the race. I think what set me apart from other runners wasn't that I was better than most but rather that I was always trying to maximize my potential and, in doing so, often helped pull others along to their personal bests.

When I ran the 2011 Boston Marathon, I pulled the field along for most of the first twenty miles at world record pace. Despite my time being fast enough to win the race any other year of the 115 years the Boston Marathon has been running, I didn't win the race. That day, I finished fourth. Yet I will always remember crossing the finishing line that year with a sense of accomplishment, joy, and excitement as I clapped my hands in celebration and let out a yell of exhilaration.

Even though I finished in fourth place and easily could have been miffed that I'd run so fast yet had not won or made the podium, I felt as happy as if I had won the race. Not only had I run a marathon faster than I'd ever run before, but I'd also exceeded what I'd thought was possible for me to run in the Boston Marathon.

I have found that the best way to compete is to strive for personal excellence. I always performed at my best when I wasn't trying to beat others or even beat my best performance but instead was trying to get everything I could out of my body on that particular day. Not only that, but I also was most successful when I was pushing others to run better than they otherwise could. Competition can be a beautiful thing if we are focused on making ourselves and others better and are not concerned about how we stack up with everyone else. When we compete in the right way, we can find satisfaction in our performances, no matter where we finish, because our goal has been to maximize what we could do that day. I always find it sad when Olympians, getting interviewed after winning a silver medal, are asked by a reporter, "Are you disappointed you didn't win the gold?" This athlete has just finished second in the world and yet they are expected to feel disappointed with this lifetime achievement because someone else was a little better. This is why comparisons in athletics and in life are so fruitless. When we compare, we miss the joy of the journey as well as the joy of achievement. Even those few who reach the pinnacle of their sport, business, or other pursuit often end up disappointed when they finally get to the top. It isn't uncommon for Olympic gold medalists to suffer depression shortly after their wins because if their main reason for competing is to beat others, when they achieve that, their journey is over. That is depressing!

I'll admit that competing with a heart of excellence instead of an attitude of comparison is a difficult perspective to develop and hold on to, but it brings so much life, joy, and satisfaction to your pursuits that it's worth the hard work to develop such a heart. Romans 12:2 says to be "transformed by the renewing of your mind," and there couldn't be a truer encouragement for those of us who are going after a heart of excellence. Even after I had changed my mindset, I still felt myself slipping back into disappointment if I didn't win a race or beat my best time, but this disappointment always triggered me to ask, "Why am I competing—to compare myself with others or with my performances, or to pursue excellence?"

I've learned that I must always remind myself of what I am going after and, even more than that, to remember God's words: "You follow Me." Use others to draw out your best, but also be that person for others. You will find your pursuits deeply rewarding, no matter what the outcome. When we compare, we lose. Comparison sucks the life out of what we are doing. We are all on a beautiful journey, so let us be thankful for every step, even if our journey looks different from someone else's.

Celebration

I had just competed in the 2007 London Marathon and set an American debut record of 2:08:24 in my first-ever marathon. With that performance, I was the favorite going into the Olympic Trials, even though it would be the first Olympic Trials I had competed in. I had spent the summer in Europe because Sara was racing the summer track circuit there, and my training had been going well. After Europe, I headed back home to Mammoth Lakes, California, to begin my specific marathon training block, which is typically twelve weeks long.

In training, you want your body to feel like a sponge. You want to feel like you are absorbing all of the hard training, and you should be noticing that your workouts are slowly getting better. But my workouts were trending in the opposite direction. They seemed to be slowly sliding backward, and I was beginning to be unable to finish workouts because of extreme fatigue, which was rare for me, because I always finished workouts. This went on for a couple of weeks before my coach, Terrence Mahon, decided I needed to take three days off, which for me—with the Olympic Trials looming—felt like taking three months off.

During those three days, depression crept in. I was home alone because Sara was still racing in Europe. Bored because I wasn't training, I began to feel that I wasn't going to be ready for the Trials. I recall talking on the phone with Sara during that time and telling her, "There is no way I'm making this team." I had been running terribly and now I wasn't even training, plus I was depressed. To make matters worse, when I got depressed, I often sought out pleasures to make myself feel better, which usually came in the form of food. I spent three days eating everything in sight and lying on the couch trying to collect myself and get out of my ever-expanding pit of despair. Giving in to that vice made me feel even more defeated, and to be honest, I didn't feel like God was encouraging me or helping me despite my prayers asking that He would.

Then on the third day, just before dark, I felt the Holy Spirit leading me to go for a run. Because I had about ten pounds of food in my gut and was in a bad spot mentally, running was the last thing I felt like doing. Yet somehow I found the strength to reluctantly lace up my shoes and head out the door to a peaceful trail that wove through a meadow. During my short run, I felt like the Holy Spirit was telling me, "I want you to celebrate like you just won the Olympic Trials." My response was something like, "Are you serious?!" In my emotional and physical state, I couldn't have been farther from feeling like celebrating. Yet again I forced myself to obey, so all by myself out in that meadow, I threw my arms in the air and ran in celebration. As soon as I did this, I felt something shift and my depression began to lift. My circumstances hadn't changed. I had probably gained five pounds in three days, which, as you can imagine, wasn't the best thing for a marathoner. I still felt fatigued, but my heart was starting to regain the hope it had lost.

When I got home from that run, I felt like the Holy Spirit

was prompting me to go to church. At the time, Sara and I attended a small but amazing church in Mammoth called the Lighthouse. There was a guest preacher that day, and before he began his sermon, he called me out and had me stand up because he had a word from God for me. This was the first time something like this had ever happened to me, so I felt a little nervous and uncomfortable. The guest preacher said he felt like God was speaking Psalm 20:4–5 to me: "May He grant you your heart's desire and fulfill all your counsel! We will sing for joy over your victory, and in the name of our God we will set up our banners. May the LORD fulfill all your petitions."

You would think that, at these powerful words and considering my circumstances, my spirit would have jumped inside of me and I would have felt hope coursing like electricity through my veins, but that wasn't my response. Instead, I thought, *You have no idea how far gone I am. There isn't a chance in the world of that happening!* It was a strange thought to have, considering I had just returned from a run in which I had celebrated winning the Olympic Trials, but that was my honest reaction. Even though I had gotten a little bit of hope on my run, I wasn't full of faith yet. Despite my negative reaction to the encouraging word, though, I continued to feel the shift that was slowly happening in my spirit. More than that, I felt like even though I didn't have the faith to partner with the word I had been given, I could align myself with the faith of someone who did believe in God's power to change my heart and my body.

The following morning, I resumed training. While I didn't see a dramatic shift in the quality of my workouts, things were slowly trending better. And when I was training, that was what I was looking for—gradual improvement over a long period of time. Each week, I was getting stronger, but I was still nowhere near race-sharp. I didn't run one tune-up race prior to the Olympic Trials, which is uncommon in marathon running, so I had absolutely no idea what kind of shape I was in. My workouts had been solid, but they weren't the best they had ever been. Consequently, my confidence was far from soaring when I arrived in New York City for the Trials.

When the race started, we settled into a comfortable pace with pretty much all of the more than one hundred runners all tightly packed together. The race progressed in this way until, somewhere around the six-mile mark, someone threw in a light surge to test everyone. I, along with about five other runners, responded but was surprised when a gap opened to separate us from the field, because we were still not running all that fast. Our group of five contained all the favorites, and we continued to run in this fashion as we completed circle after circle around Central Park.

I remember thinking that this felt like a planking competition instead of a road race. All of us were looking around, wondering who would be the first to fold and which three of us would end up making the Olympic team. With one lap (six miles) to go, we circled past the finishing line and I looked up at the jumbotron that was streaming the race. The screen was split between one camera focused on our pack and another camera focused on Khalid Khannouchi, who was the biggest wild card in the race. At one time, Khalid had held the world record in the marathon, with a time almost three minutes faster than anyone else's in the Trials field. I heard the announcer remark that Khalid was closing the gap on our lead group, which made me eager to pick up the pace so as not to allow such a talented runner back in the race. I made what felt to me like a slight pickup in speed, attempting to put some distance between myself and Khalid, but apparently it was a bigger surge than I'd thought, because the gap between me and the others in the lead pack expanded. I knew this was my time to go. I'd learned over the years that when you have the energy to pick up the pace, you need to use it right away, because it doesn't always come back.

Even though it felt like it was too early to open up a gap, I followed the energy my body was giving me and kept increasing the pace. I was surprised to see my splits going down from roughly five-minute miles to closer to 4:40 miles. And I was also surprised by how I felt. I had been feeling solid but not great, but with my surge, I started feeling better and better. In those last six miles, I felt like I experienced a little piece of heaven. It was as if the faster I ran, the better I felt. I'll never forget the sensation, but what I remember most was feeling the presence of God in such a tangible way, so much so that I felt the hairs on my arms standing up. I've had a handful of times in my running career when I felt like I experienced God's presence strongly inside me, and this moment was probably the strongest.

What was so special about that race wasn't the performance, even though I lived out my dream of qualifying for the Beijing Olympics, in an Olympic Trials record time of 2:09:02. It was, instead, the connection I felt with God during the race. In those last couple of miles, as reserved as I tend to be, I could not hold my celebration back any longer. I ran those last miles yelling "Praise God!" and shouting for joy. It was outside of my personality to have such an exuberant celebration, but it was a celebration not only of my God-given destiny being fulfilled but also of the encounter I was having with God. I can relate to how David may have felt when he ripped off his clothes and danced before the ark of the covenant.

I remember watching the video replay of the finish during the afterparty and awards ceremony and being more than slightly embarrassed by the degree of my celebration, but in that moment it had to come out. Funny to think, if you had played a video of the race to me three months earlier when I was deep in depression and gorging on food, I wouldn't have believed that such a race was possible, and it likely *wouldn't* have been possible had it not been for God's encouraging me to celebrate before my victory. It also wouldn't have been possible without the faith of another to share and stand with me in the truth that, with God, we are always victorious, even if we don't win the race.

When I'm going through tough times, I like to imagine my future self encouraging my current self. It says in Psalm 2:4, "He who sits in the heavens laughs." I think perhaps the reason God is able to laugh at life's circumstances is because He knows what is going to happen in the end. He sees the whole picture. As Paul says in Romans 8:18, "For I consider that the sufferings of this present time are not worthy to be compared with the glory that is to be revealed to us." When we are battling tough circumstances or fighting depression, we need to ask God to show us the end. The Bible says that we are sitting in the heavenly realms (see Eph. 2:6), so we have access to this future knowledge much in the same way that the guest preacher had access to a prophetic word over my future. God may not give us a video play-by-play, but He can restore our focus on the big picture instead of on the small, day-to-day happenings that can trip us up. And the more we partner with God to see our circumstances the way He sees them, the more hope we are filled with and the more empowered we will be to live our destiny.

After I won the Olympic Trials, my hometown of Big Bear

Lake took such pride in my victory and subsequent spot on the Olympic team that they hung a massive, thirty-foot banner with a picture of me on the main street of town. In the picture, I'm holding up one finger and pointing to God, which could also be seen as my saying, "I'm number one!" I knew the true meaning of the image, though, and whenever I saw it, I was drawn back to my encounter with God. I knew exactly why I was pointing to the sky. And I laughed at how literally the word was fulfilled: "We will sing for joy over your victory, and in the name of God we will set up our banners."

Unoffendable

It was almost the day I had been dreaming about since I was thirteen years old, back when God had placed the call on my life to run with the best runners in the world. As I was doing my customary premarathon thirty-minute easy jog around a 1,000 meter woodchip trail in the Olympic Village in Beijing, China, my mind wandered ahead to the next day. What would the day hold? Would it be the day I had dreamed of my entire life, and would I have my best race ever? Would God show up and strengthen my body in supernatural ways? I directed my curiosity toward God and asked Him a simple question: "What would you like to tell me in preparation for tomorrow?"

Immediately, the story of Shadrach, Meshach, and Abednego came rushing into my mind. I had read the story many times of the three young men who refused to worship the king's gods and were thrown into a fiery furnace, a furnace so hot that the guards who threw them in were consumed by the flames. Yet God showed up and delivered the three and was even seen by the king as He was walking among them in the fire. I was hoping that God gave me this story because He was about to deliver me from the fiery furnace I would face in the extremely hot and humid Beijing summer, but I needed to dig deeper than that to find the meaning.

As is my custom when I am running and hear something from God, afterward I like to spend additional time with God with a Bible in hand and a notepad as I read the Word and discuss with God why He is highlighting it to me. As I reread the passage, I was struck by a part I'd never focused on: "Shadrach, Meshach and Abed-nego replied to the king, 'O Nebuchadnezzar, we do not need to give you an answer concerning this matter. If it be so, our God whom we serve is able to deliver us from the furnace of blazing fire; and He will deliver us out of your hand, O king. But even if He does not, let it be known to you, O king, that we are not going to serve your gods or worship the golden image that you have set up'" (Dan. 3:16–18).

What really hit me wasn't so much the young men's confidence that God would deliver them but rather their steadfastness to God, independent of whether He showed up. They had hearts that were unoffendable toward God. Their devotion, love, and affection toward God could not be broken by results. No matter what God chose to do and no matter whether they liked His decision, nothing could change their hearts toward Him. I was amazed and inspired by their attitude and their strength. And I realized that I too must develop and cultivate the same unoffendable heart. I decided that even if the opposite of my dreams came to pass, nothing was going to affect my heart toward God. This decision was put to the test less than twenty-four hours later.

I woke up race day to the craziest storm I'd ever seen in my life. It was still dark at this early morning hour, but I had been tossing and turning, anxiously awaiting the alarm to go off so I could begin my prerace rituals. The first thing I would always do is go to the window and look outside, attempting to gauge the weather conditions, especially the wind. Being a frontrunner, I hated running in the wind, so I was always hoping to see a flag lying calmly or a tree with its branches perfectly still. What I saw on this morning, though, kept me standing at the window for longer than a brief glance. Lightning was striking in the dawning sky with such repetitiveness that it looked like a time-lapse video of a storm. I stood at the window, awed by the impressive lightning and downpouring of rain, and then suddenly the storm stopped. As if on command, the sky began to clear. I still don't know what happened, but there had been talk of the Chinese Olympic Committee "seeding the clouds" in the hope of causing a rainstorm that would clear the polluted air. I'm guessing that this is what was going on, because I've never seen a storm like it.

After the weather check, I continued my prerace rituals: drinking twenty ounces of water upon waking, consuming my shake of CytoCarb (maltodextrin, which is a complex yet easy to digest carbohydrate) and Muscle Milk protein, and then of course having my race-day coffee. Caffeine may be a daily ritual for some, but for me coffee was reserved strictly for its performance benefits, which meant that I consumed it only three days a week, exactly an hour or an hour and a half prior to a race or a hard workout. I had packed in my luggage two hot water boilers (just in case I had a malfunction when trying to make hot water), my French press, and a brand-new, unopened bag of coffee. The morning of the race, panic set in when neither hot water boiler was working and I was out of options for heating water to brew my coffee. As I pondered the idea of chewing my coffee grounds, my friend and longtime teammate (and also my roommate in the Olympic

Village) Ian popped in to see if I needed anything. Perfect timing! Ian relieved my building stress by running to the massive cafeteria and grabbing enough hot water for me to brew with. Things were looking up as, with coffee in hand and not a cloud in the sky, I hopped on the bus that would take us to the warmup area.

As my fellow US teammates in the marathon, Dathan Ritzenhein and Brian Sell, and I warmed up for the race, the sun crept higher and higher into the sky. The heat and humidity were elevated, but the morning's storm had cleared the air of pollution, and I could see the sky and the sun for the first time since arriving in Beijing. With all the hype about the heat, the focus of most of the prerace talk was on how slow the winning time likely would be. Running in heat and humidity adds minutes to an elite marathoner's time, and our coaches and staff, knowing how running in such conditions drain the body, were encouraging us to dial back the pace early on. We all assumed that the race would start slowly and most likely be won in a time much slower than any of our personal bests.

My least favorite part of running has always been standing at the starting line of a race. It's like looking down the barrel of a loaded rifle. You know what awaits you, but there's nothing you can do about it. Once the gun fires, it's as if a giant balloon of nervousness has been shot and I'm finally released to go into battle. When the gun fired in Beijing, it was as if everyone on the starting line got hit with an uppercut by a Kenyan athlete named Sammy Wanjiru, who ran the opening miles in a shockingly fast pace. None of us expected the race to start as fast as it did, so everyone scrambled to react and shift our mindset from running slow to opening up the race at Olympic Marathon record pace. That day I was reminded of a valuable lesson my coach had told me: "Adopt the saying of the Samurai: 'expect nothing, be ready for everything.'" In the early miles, I found myself in the middle of the pack, with the leaders already having a substantial lead over me. This wasn't my plan, because I knew that the winner—and likely the other medalists—would come from the lead pack. But I had no choice. I simply wasn't fit enough to run so fast in such challenging conditions.

I had raced Sammy and many of the other top contenders a few months earlier in the London Marathon. I had finished fifth in that race, but I'd hung with the leaders the entire way until the last few miles. I knew I had a shot at a medal in Beijing, but I needed to have a great day. With such lofty goals and expectations, I didn't like sitting so far back with an ever-growing gap to the leaders. It was extremely discouraging.

One of the best pieces of advice I'd ever received about running a marathon came from Deena Kastor, my teammate and Olympic silver medalist in the Athens Olympic Marathon. Deena told me that you go through both good and bad patches in a marathon, so when you're going through a bad patch, you need to keep fighting, because eventually you will come out on the other side. I was hoping that my first 10K in Beijing was just a bad patch and that I would somehow find the strength to close the gap on the leaders, whom I could no longer see down the long, winding roads in front of me. I kept trying to coach myself through the early stages of the race: "You're not hot. You're running great! Just do your best. You can get back in this race—just be patient." But even with all that positive self-talk, I wasn't able to ward off the frustration I felt.

I began to pray as I ran. I asked God for the wisdom and strength to endure the "fiery furnace" that seemed to be burning me up. And what I heard God answer was, "Encourage others." Now, encouraging other runners was the last thing I felt like doing. I had been hoping for a medal, and here I was back around sixtieth place, feeling hot, tired, and irritable. But I've learned—and am still learning—that when God tells you to do something, it is because He is a good Dad who knows what's best for you. So I found something encouraging to say to every guy I caught and passed, which isn't typically done among elite marathoners. Most runners will surge hard when they pass a runner to break their spirit and discourage them. That's what you do if your goal is to beat people. But there isn't any comparison in the kingdom of God. There's only loving others, which involves wanting the best for them and even seeking to help them reach new levels of excellence. So it was in line with God's perspective that God was telling me to encourage other runners.

As I did so, my mind finally got outside of myself. I was no longer focused on how poorly I was performing, how hot I was, or how frustrated I felt. I was simply focused on trying to help the guys around me. To be honest, I knew at the halfway point that barring a miracle, my dream of standing on the podium was over. I still believed that God could perform a physical miracle, but what I didn't realize at the time was that He was performing a miracle inside of me. He was using me to bring His kingdom—the kingdom that is inside every believer—into the Olympic Marathon, and by running with such a heart, I was making my spirit stronger, which led to my body performing better.

I'll be honest. Most of the time when I ask God for a miracle, I want a physical miracle. I sometimes tend to see miracles of the heart as second-rate miracles, but that couldn't be farther from the truth. The truth is, a miracle that happens in the physical is amazing, but it won't last forever, whereas a miracle that happens in your heart, if cultivated, will last for a lifetime.

As I continued to encourage other runners, I found myself relaxing and catching more and more guys. I experienced the truth that when we encourage others, we ourselves will be encouraged. ("The generous man will be prosperous, and he who waters will himself be watered," Prov. 11:25). By the twenty-mile mark, I had worked myself up into the top twenty, but the leaders were still nowhere in sight. Now the problem I was facing was that the gaps between runners were growing larger, which meant that I was spending more time running by myself. With nobody around me to encourage, feelings of discouragement and frustration worked their way back into my heart and mind.

When the Bird's Nest (the Olympic stadium) came into view, it was a welcome sight. I was ready to be done. I'd worked my way up to tenth place, but that wasn't what I had hoped for when I'd imagined God rescuing me from the fiery furnace. The interesting thing is that though I couldn't see it at the time, God was very much with me in that race, and He really did help me endure the furnace through His advice to encourage the people around me. Like He was with Shadrach, Meshach, and Abed-nego, God was in the furnace and walking with me, rescuing me from the flames of shattered dreams, hopes, aspirations, and expectations.

Competing in an Olympic Marathon is an amazing experience. Imagine an entire 26.2 mile course filled with screaming fans as you run through the streets of a major city. The noise was deafening at times, causing me to get goosebumps as I ran. This certainly had been the case in Beijing until I hit the tunnel leading into the Olympic stadium, where all I could hear was the pitter-patter of my feet. Here I was running into the Olympic stadium—a moment I'd been dreaming of my entire life—and yet I didn't want to be there, not like this anyway. I had devoted my life to my craft, and I had done it to get an Olympic medal, not tenth place. But a funny thing happened when I entered the tunnel and everything got quiet. I felt God speaking to me again, and this time He was saying, "This isn't everything you dreamed of, but this is everything you need." At that moment, I knew I could trust that even when things don't go as I'd hoped they would, God knows what is best for me, and whatever He gives me is good for me.

It was with this mindset that I dealt with my offense toward God for His not showing up in the way I wanted Him to. I still don't fully understand why things played out the way they did that day, but I can clearly see how close and present God was as I endured the flames that threatened to consume me. I could have walked away from my first Olympic experience bitter, frustrated, heartbroken, and angry at God, but He was in the furnace with me, helping me navigate the rocky road faced by all Olympic athletes who find themselves finishing off the podium.

I'm glad God got ahold of me in that tunnel, because that day, He changed my heart. I went into the tunnel as a frustrated, pouting man, and I came out of it as a grateful one, ready to soak up the experience of crossing the Olympic Marathon finishing line. That moment remains one of the most precious memories of my career. I'll never forget the sound of thousands of feet stomping on the ground above as I worked my way through the tunnel, or the amazing sight I saw when I exited the tunnel and entered the stadium—people of every nation, together making one roar of sound in celebration. It's how I imagine heaven will be. I'll never forget running past my family members who had made the long trip to watch me compete in the Olympics. I waved to them as I ran by, as if to say, "Thank you for coming on this journey with me and making this moment possible." I wanted to show them that even though I hadn't done what I'd hoped to do, my heart was still intact and I was going to be okay.

I'd like to be able to tell you that in the wake of the Beijing Olympic Marathon, I never battled frustration or discouragement again, but that wouldn't be true. Waves of discouragement hit me from time to time through the following months, but I always came back to what God taught me about being unoffendable toward Him as I trusted in His goodness. Removing my expectations of how I want God to show up and shifting my eyes toward what God is doing in and around me is a daily goal, because I see this as the primary way I can be thankful to God rather than offended toward Him. I have learned to trust that God is a good Father who always has my best interests at heart. Whether or not He delivers me from the flames in a physical way, I can always trust Him and adopt the same attitude as Shadrach, Meshach, and Abed-nego and, no matter what happens, have a heart that is unoffendable toward Him.

Pain

Often I described my job as a professional runner as being a professional pain manager. That's how it felt when I was twenty miles into a marathon and everything in my body was on fire and I still had more than six miles of hard running to go. I vividly remember being at the top of the Boston Marathon's famed Heartbreak Hill and thinking, *There has got to be an easier way to make a living than this!* Despite the pain, I usually could manage to focus on what felt good, rather than focusing on all the muscles that were screaming at me to stop, a tactic I learned from my dad when I was getting into the sport. I could always tell when I didn't have much left—my forearms would start to hurt, and that was usually the last muscle group to give out. I often felt that the level to which I could perform was determined by the amount of pain I could overcome. Thus, much of my running career was spent learning to overcome pain.

I tried a lot of strategies to push harder when confronted with immense pain. I tried listening to really loud music when I ran. I tried focusing on my goals. I tried telling myself over and over that I needed to push myself harder than I'd ever pushed before. I tried reverse psychology, attempting to convince myself that I loved pain. I tried reciting Bible verses, praying, focusing on the positive. I even tried to zone out, emptying my mind in an attempt not to think about the pain. Some of these strategies were effective to a certain level—and they rightfully have their place in the business of pain management—but the most effective way for me to manage my pain was something I discovered much later in my career.

When I was running, I often felt myself wondering how Jesus was able to handle the unimaginable pain He experienced on the cross. I found myself asking God how to handle pain, and eventually I felt He led me to Hebrews 12:1–2: "Therefore, since we have so great a cloud of witnesses surrounding us, let us also lay aside every encumbrance and the sin which so easily entangles us, and let us run with endurance the race that is set before us, fixing our eyes on Jesus, the author and perfecter of faith, who for the joy set before Him endured the cross, despising the shame, and has sat down at the right hand of the throne of God."

I found this passage to be an answer for how to handle suffering. "For the joy set before Him" was the best way for Jesus to overcome pain, and it is also the best way for us to overcome our suffering. We overcome pain by finding joy. But how do we find joy while we're suffering? These seem like two very different—contradictory, even—experiences. And what was this joy that Jesus had set before Him? I'm not sure anyone on earth knows the answer to these questions, but I believe the joy that Jesus had set before Him was His love for you, me, and all of humanity, and what His death would accomplish for us.

Jesus' mission on earth was to restore humanity to God. When He gave up His spirit on the cross, He called out, "It is finished" (John 19:30), and all of humanity now had access to God through Jesus' blood, as was made evident by the tearing of the veil in the holy of holies (Mark 15:38). I can't help but wonder if, when Jesus was being whipped or was having a nail hammered through His hand, a picture of you or me flashed through His mind. I believe that when Jesus was hanging on the cross, He was able to find joy that was rooted in His love for us, joy that allowed Him to overcome incredible pain. The more I understood this, the more I realized that I needed to find the same joy and motivation for overcoming my pain.

I love that the author of this passage says that the way to increase our endurance is to "fix our eyes on Jesus." It's logical to think that if Jesus pictured us as He hung on the cross, then we can overcome our pain by fixing our eyes on Him. To my mind, no one articulates this line of thinking as well as Dietrich Bonhoeffer does in his book *The Cost of Discipleship*. Bonhoeffer says that we shouldn't look down the road ahead at what is too hard for us, but rather we should set our eyes on Jesus, who is right in front of us, and say, "He leads the way; I will follow." I remember being at mile six of the London Marathon and feeling my calves prematurely tightening up on me. I started thinking about how many miles I still had to go, but fortunately I was able to channel my thinking and instead focus on just running the mile I was in and ended up running a personal best of 2:06:17. Had I continued to think about how hard the road was going to be, I never would have made it. The truth is that the road was hard, but the greater truth is that God always supplies, by His grace, all the strength we need for each moment to accomplish His purposes.

Grace for the moment is the key to endurance. Grace is the supernatural power given by God to overcome in a situation, and the one who gives us this grace, Jesus, is right in front of us, in whatever moment we are in. Becoming a parent is a perfect example of how this works. Before Sara and I had our own kids and were feeling nervous about adopting, almost every parent we talked to said they didn't feel ready for their first kid, but when the child arrived, they always found they had the grace to endure each moment, no matter how difficult. It may not be the strength to win the race in the world's eyes—or even in our own eyes, if our definition of winning isn't in line with God's—but God always gives us the grace and strength to follow Him and accomplish His purpose in every situation. That is the true definition of winning.

Bad things happen when we look too far down a hard road. I always tell people that my least favorite part of a marathon is standing on the starting line, because it's so easy to partner with fear when you're anticipating the many painful miles that lie ahead. I need to remind myself to just run the mile I'm in. Forget about how hard the hill at mile twenty is going to be, forget about the pain I'm going to feel at mile twenty-five, because on the starting line, I don't yet have the grace to handle the hill at mile twenty or the pain of mile twenty-five. I only have the grace to handle the moment I'm in, so I need to stay present with Jesus, fixing my eyes on Him so I can endure the pain.

In 2009, I was competing in my first New York City Marathon and had pledged to donate any prize money I won to our newly established Hall Steps Foundation, which takes steps to eliminate extreme poverty, specifically in East Africa. I was in the best running shape of my life. I remember doing an eighteen-mile run on a hilly course in Mammoth Lakes at exactly a five-minute-mile pace at nearly eight thousand feet altitude. I had never been so fit. My expectations for the race were high, and I was dreaming about bringing home a sizeable paycheck to donate to our foundation. I knew that a six-figure prize could change thousands and thousands of lives in the projects with which we were partnering, which became a powerful motivator.

The race started and I settled into the lead group, which I remained in through the halfway mark, but something was amiss. I just wasn't feeling it that day. Running can be a mystery—sometimes you're in the best shape of your life, but for no apparent reason, you just don't have it on race day. Despite having one of those off days, though, at halfway I was still in the pack and still in the hunt to bring home good prize money for Steps. Shortly after the halfway mark, we hit First Avenue, and anyone who is familiar with the NYC Marathon knows that on First Avenue, things get crazy. It's slightly downhill, and the crowds are massive and loud, so all the runners feel a major surge of adrenaline. Left unchecked, this adrenaline high can lead to running a lot faster than you think you are as well as faster than you should, creating big problems once the adrenaline wears off. This year was no different, and I was a casualty of First Avenue, not because I surged too hard but rather because I couldn't go with the group when they increased the pace, resulting in my drifting outside of the top ten. I remember running down First Avenue after the lead pack had dropped me, thinking, *I know how to get back to the hotel from here. Maybe I'll just rip off my number and cut off the course to avoid the suffering of those last eleven miles.* Honestly that was the thought running through my mind, but then I thought about why I was racing. I wasn't running for myself. I was running to win funds for and to create awareness of those who live in extreme poverty. I began to see pictures of the kids in Zambia I had visited, kids who wore tattered clothes and owned nothing. Sara and I had recently met these kids on a trip with Team World Vision, an organization we partnered with in fundraising to bring clean water to ninety thousand community members. After our trip, our hearts were impacted and we wanted to do more by starting our own foundation to support organizations like World Vision that were doing sustainable effective work.

As I thought about those I was running for and stopped focusing on my pain, disappointment, and discouragement, my body relaxed. When I got outside of my suffering by focusing on loving others, what happened in my heart slowly manifested in the physical realm. My body started functioning properly again. I picked up the pace without even trying. This is a huge lesson I've learned when attempting to overcome pain: trying harder doesn't help. Often, it feels like the harder I try, the worse I perform. I've had to learn to let my performances flow out of my body rather than try to force them to happen. It's all about having the mentality that my best performance *wants* to come out, and all I have to do is let it come out. If I force it, my body will not cooperate. My best performance will come only when my body is relaxed. Perhaps that's what happens when in the midst of our suffering, we focus on our love for others and our love for God, and that love causes us to relax.

Over the last eleven miles of the NYC Marathon, instead of enduring a slow and painful run, I worked my way up to finish just behind the third-place runner, bringing home a nice payday for Steps. That never would have happened had I not stopped dwelling on my pain and started focusing on others. After that, I began to think about those I loved whenever I raced. If I was in the lead pack of a race, I would look into the TV camera and picture those I loved watching me compete, or I would picture God watching me run with a smile on His face, or I would picture the faces of some of the children I'd met whom I was running to help. I found that the most powerful tool for overcoming pain is to be motivated by love.

There's an experiment you can do where you hold your arm out straight to the side and someone tells you to think about someone or something you hate while they push your arm down to see how much strength you have to resist. Then they repeat the experiment, but the second time they tell you to think of something or someone you love. The result is astounding. The degree of strength you have when thinking of love is so much greater than the strength that comes from hatred. That's why athletes who compete because they really want to beat someone are never maximizing their potential. Competing out of love results in superior strength. The next time you find yourself in a painful situation, find a way outside of yourself. Think about your love for God, your family, your friends, those you are helping. There is more strength inside of you than you can imagine when you fix your eyes on Jesus. All you have to do is stay close and stay in love, and you can endure incredible pain.

As a marathon prerace ritual, I often watched *The Passion of the Christ* before going to bed on the eve of a race. It's a graphic movie, but it always burned the face of Jesus into my mind, which made it easier for me to picture Him as I was competing the next day. Whatever it is for you that gets the picture of Jesus in your mind is a great way to prepare for the hard journey ahead. Then, when it feels like the pain is encompassing you, go into your mind's eye and picture the suffering Christ on the cross, who was thinking of how much He loves you. Letting our hearts and minds fill with love is the most powerful tool we have to push through pain and find the true limits of our bodies.

Faith

In the fall of 2010, I decided to leave my coach and my training group in Mammoth Lakes to begin what I called faith-based coaching. I began this journey because I sincerely believe that God has all the answers to everything in life, with no exceptions—even how best to train for the marathon. I was also desperate to experience God in a real way. I found that my life had become very comfortable, and though I was in relationship with God, I hadn't been desperate to experience more of Him. Stepping out and depending on Him as my coach would force me to seek Him and experience Him every day.

This decision was unorthodox for a professional athlete and one that took much prayer and processing with Sara and others whom I respected. After much consideration, in the fall of 2010 I decided to have God as my coach. It would have been easier to live out this faith-based experiment in a bubble, but being the best marathoner in the US didn't afford me that opportunity. My decision became the subject of public discussion, which as with all other media about me, I tried not to pay attention to.

When I began faith-based coaching, I felt like I was leaving everything behind. In a sense, I was, because I left my coach, my team, and my home in Mammoth Lakes to follow a path I felt God calling me to. I assumed I would turn into somewhat of a running monk, logging hundreds of solitary miles, just me and God, but this wasn't at all what happened. The first lesson God taught me as my coach is that greatness comes forth from community. As soon as I left it all behind, God led me to various experts to assist me on my journey. He led me to a friend, Billy Herman, who was willing to pace me on a bike for all of my workouts. He led me to move to Flagstaff, Arizona, so I could be close to one of the top sports therapists, John Ball, who regularly restored my beaten-down body to wholeness. God then led me to talk to various coaches who offered me training advice, along with many others who aided me greatly on my journey. I was made whole and better through the community God surrounded me with. Sometimes when I think of following God, I just imagine it as Him and me and no one else, but I have learned that this isn't the correct view. Following God looks like learning to live in community so we can make each other better. It was never meant to be a lone-soldier journey. If we are going to attain our full potential in anything, we need the support of community to get there.

When I started out with God as my coach, I would sit down with a pen and paper and ask Him questions. This was a bit of a transition for me, because my prayer times were usually more like my talking at God than my giving Him space to speak back. But I've discovered that if I'm not asking God questions, I'm not creating room to hear Him. I had been taught how to pray from the time I was a little kid in Sunday school, so I was well versed in knowing how to talk to God, and I did listen for His voice, but the concept of asking Him

specific questions and expecting to hear His answers immediately was new to me. Sure enough, though, when I started
asking Him questions, He started answering them. And one of
the first questions I asked God is, Where does strength come
from? The answer wasn't what I expected or even wanted to
hear: rest. I had always prided myself on being a workhorse,
the guy who trained harder than everyone else. My mentality
was always, *You may beat me, but you will not out-train me.* But
now I felt God leading me to a couple of verses that would
teach me about true strength:

- "For thus the Lord GOD, the Holy One of Israel, has said,
  'In repentance and rest you will be saved, in quietness
  and trust is your strength.' But you were not willing"
  (Isa. 30:15).
- "Unless the LORD builds the house, they labor in vain
  who build it; unless the LORD guards the city, the watch-
  man keeps awake in vain. It is vain for you to rise up
  early, to retire late, to eat bread of painful labors; for He
  gives to His beloved even in his sleep" (Ps. 127:1–2).

These verses were hard for me to practice. I found it much
harder to trust God and train less, believing that strength
comes from rest, than to train like a madman. It was a
difficult lesson to learn—that resting takes tremendous confidence and courage. I decided to take one day off per week
as a way to operate from rest, which maybe doesn't sound
like much to the everyday runner, but it was to me. I was
reducing my weekly mileage by one seventh, which seemed
like a huge amount. All of a sudden, running my customary
120-mile weeks became difficult to do with only six days of
running, so my mileage dropped closer to a hundred miles

per week. I also spaced my hard workouts out more. Instead of taking only one easy day between hard sessions, I took two, which made me question whether I was working hard enough to race as fast as I had been. Though it was hard initially to trust God and take more rest, it didn't take me long to see that operating from rest was working. And once I saw the results, I became more and more confident that God was right—strength comes from rest.

When it came to planning my daily training, I was hoping that God would give me all kinds of crazy dreams and visions of the perfect workouts I needed to be doing, but that wasn't my experience. Instead, I felt God reinforcing that He had already brought some amazing coaches into my life to teach me the foundations of training. I made some minor tweaks and occasionally did some workouts I'd never done before—like 20 by 1,000 meters with a short 200-meter jog between, and twenty-four-mile runs in which I alternated miles in five minutes with miles in six minutes for the entire run. But for the most part, I relied largely upon the workouts I had done in the past that had worked for me, only making minor adjustments that I felt God was leading me to make, such as building in more rest.

My expectation was that everything would click as I received divine training perfectly suited for my body because it was written by the one who created my body. Instead, I discovered that learning to hear from God is a lot like learning a second language. You first have to spend time listening and trying to decipher what you're hearing, and you're guaranteed to make some mistakes in the process. I'll be the first to admit that some things I thought I was hearing from God weren't coming from Him at all. For example, prior to the 2012 Olympics, I felt God was telling me that all of the pieces of the puzzle were going to come together and I was going to run my best race ever. I believed He was telling me I was going to run 4:40 per mile for the entire race. (At that point, my pace for a marathon was 4:45 miles, and taking five seconds off each mile is a large jump for a professional runner.) Quite the opposite happened, and I ended up dropping out for the first time ever because of a hamstring tear. Clearly the puzzle was not coming together. But what I strongly felt in my spirit when I stepped off the race course in London, the largest disappointment of my career thus far, was, "It's better to lose with God than to win without Him." It was as if God was encouraging me: "Yes, you did hear Me wrong, but I am still with you and always will be with you."

Proverbs 14:4 says, "Where no oxen are, the manger is clean, but much revenue comes by the strength of the ox." Taking risks is messy, and mine had created a big mess, but it is by taking risks that we experience the power of God. Hearing from God is like anything else in this life—it takes practice, and most likely we're going to get it wrong from time to time—but failure shouldn't discourage us from hearing His voice and lead us to just settle for a clean manger. Failure to hear God correctly should just be instructional and lead us to more accurately hear Him in the future.

One of the greatest lessons I learned about hearing God's voice had to do with my heart condition in both training and racing: *how* you do what you do is more important than *what* you do. When I switched to faith-based training, I was concerned about what workout I was going to do that day, whereas God was concerned about what was going on in my heart while I was doing the workout. I feel like this is often the case with us and God—we're concerned about what is happening on the outside, while He's concerned about what is happening on the inside. Perhaps this is because He knows we live out of our hearts. This is why we are instructed, "Above all else, guard your heart, for everything you do flows from it" (Prov. 4:23 NIV).

God started speaking to me about my heart condition while I was in the middle of my training. For example, a typical workout was six repetitions of one mile with two minutes' rest between. Now, I could run this workout with a heart of proving to myself that I am fit and ready to race, in which case I would press every interval, trying to cut every second I could from each mile split, going deep into my "well of strength." It would be a race-level effort rather than a workout-level effort. Or I could go into the workout secure in who I was, trusting that God would give me the strength I needed when the race came and not try to prove anything, not pressing every interval and instead running at the correct level of effort. Running with a heart secure in who I am allowed me to find the sweet spot for my body. I was often told by my coaches not to "leave my race on the track," meaning not to exert myself so much in training that I don't have the reserves needed for race day. I always struggled to heed this advice because of my insecurity, but now, farther along in my journey and more secure in my identity, I was finally able to work out without pressing. All of this is to say that even if God had given me a vision of a sheet of paper with all the perfect workouts plotted on it for me to follow, if I wasn't doing them with the right heart, they wouldn't work.

Looking at race results, my journey in faith-based coaching might seem to be an unsuccessful experiment, but that is not how I feel looking back at it. I ran my fastest marathon ever with God as my coach (2:04:58 at the 2011 Boston Marathon), qualified for my second Olympic team, and ran

2:08 on a warm day at the Chicago Marathon. But when training for the 2012 Olympic Trials, I came down with plantar fasciitis and had no choice but to run through it to qualify. As I compensated for the pain in my foot, my stride changed. My next injury came in the Olympic Marathon with the hamstring tear, followed by a string of compensatory injuries that for two years kept me from toeing the line in another marathon. I was finally able to stay healthy going into the 2014 Boston Marathon, but I had my slowest marathon performance of my career. I found that the farther away I got from being in top form, the harder it was to get it back. Then I struggled with extreme fatigue, which led to my retirement from professional running in January 2016.

It might appear that the last years of my career proved that having God has my coach was unsuccessful, but I would counter that having God as my coach is what helped me navigate and endure the most difficult season of my running. Every athlete reaches the point where their body gives out or just can't perform at the same level it once did. That's just the truth about being a professional athlete, as well as the truth about the aging process. During this crucial time, I needed the daily perspective God gave me so that I could have the strength to handle the injuries, setbacks, fatigue, and, ultimately, retirement. And I needed God with me because I was always afraid of the day I would announce my retirement from professional running. This sport was my craft, my passion, and my life for twenty years, and I wasn't sure I could stop it without having at least a small mental breakdown. I was concerned about my sense of well-being once I retired. But what I found is that all the lessons God had taught me along my running journey, along with His leading as my coach as I went through my physical slide, gave me the grace I needed to transition well.

I'm grateful that I experienced that season of having God as my coach. He taught me many lessons that will stay with me for the rest of my life. But what I value most is how it deepened my relationship with Him. I am thankful for the time I spent asking Him questions and listening for His answers. I didn't do a perfect job of hearing His voice or following His lead, but I did experience more of God than I'd experienced before, which was my original goal and so much more fulfilling than any performance I could have achieved. I understand that God's call in my life to have Him as my coach was a specific step for me, but I believe that all of us can benefit from involving God in every part of our lives. I believe God deeply cares about every aspect of our lives and wants to give us insights, keys, and wisdom if only we will ask Him.

Worship

Coming into the 2012 Olympic Marathon Trials in Houston, Texas, I was in a different spot than when I won the 2007 Olympic Trials in NYC. I had just completed two of my best races ever, having run 2:04 in Boston that spring and then 2:08 in Chicago on a warm fall day. I'd already been to one Olympic Games, so I wasn't feeling as much pressure to become an Olympian, but I also really wanted to improve on my tenth place finish at Beijing. But my training buildup hadn't been remarkable.

After years of running the marathon, my workouts were a good indicator of how fit I was. I usually had a pretty good idea what was possible when I was standing on the starting line, but I always tried to have an open mind and believe that anything is possible with God (Luke 1:37). I figured I was probably in about 2:08 shape in Houston, based on my being able to do a fifteen-mile tempo run close to a 4:50 per mile pace at sea level. A big challenge I faced heading into this Olympic Trials was coming down with plantar fasciitis a month before (which ended up being the Achilles' heel of my running career). Every run I went on, it felt like I was being stabbed with a knife in my heel. Anyone who has had plantar fasciitis can relate, and most people have their own theory on how to fix it. You can wear a special sock with a brace in it to keep your foot flexed at night while you sleep. My dad swears by firmly wrapping the foot in duct tape. (All men are nodding their heads in agreement on this one.) You can roll your foot on a frozen juice container . . . the list goes on and on. The best advice I ever got came at the local PT's office, where I was sitting on a table getting some treatment. An old-time runner who was sitting on the table next to me also receiving treatment gave me this advice: "It's going to hurt, but eventually it will get better." Sometimes the simplest advice is also the most profound. Here I was getting laser treatment as well as every other techie treatment you can imagine, trying to get my PF under control before one of the biggest races of my life. Nothing seemed to be offering much relief from the pain, and I finally heard the words I needed to hear—that it was going to hurt for a while, and then it would get better. After I let go of the frustration, which in some ways was worse than the pain, and just accepted my situation, I felt lighter and was able to better work through the pain without the huge stress that frustration brings.

Even though physically I wasn't in the best shape, spiritually I was more connected with God than I'd ever been. Sara and I had recently relocated to Redding, California, and were auditing classes at Bethel Church's School of Supernatural Ministry. It was an amazing experience sitting in those sessions and feeling a lot of strongholds being dealt with, the biggest of which was my inclination to be so performance driven. Relearning that God didn't love me any more or any less based on how I performed in life or out on the roads was freeing.

I had been doing faith-based coaching for more than a year and was quickly learning how to hear from and connect with God. I had always experienced a spiritual connection with God when I ran, especially out in the forest by myself, but now things were different. I felt freer and lighter than I had ever felt because my connection with God was so much deeper now, resulting in my feeling more loved by God than ever. When you really experience the love of God, you can't help but go through life feeling light and free.

In the last week before the Olympic Trials race, Sara and I went to our revival group at school, where we sat in the middle of the room. One by one, about fifty students gave us encouraging words. I was wrecked—in the best possible way—by the end of that session, because what they said resonated so profoundly with who I was and what I was going after. The students had spoken of how God saw me and also of what my potential was. Every word felt like it came directly from God and encouraged me in just the way I needed encouragement before the race. My usual questioning of my fitness gave way to the greater reality that I already had the greatest prize I could attain and my value was not dependent on how well I performed at the Trials. When I feel this way, I can't help but be filled with gratitude toward God for His great love for me, and this gratitude gets expressed as worship through the act of running.

A turning point in my last week of training for the Trials came from my feeling that God was telling me I needed to rest more. Rather than sticking to my usual double-run days leading up to the Trials, I skipped all my thirty-minute afternoon runs, giving my legs more recovery time. I was amazed by the difference I felt. I went from feeling heavy legged to feeling like Tigger, bouncing along with every stride. I felt like I had springs in my legs. I believe it was listening to God's leading to take extra rest that was the difference in my making that Olympic team.

Arriving in Houston, even though my circumstances weren't what I had been hoping for with my foot injury, I felt light and free, ready to pour myself out in worship to God during the race. I'll never forget walking into a large auditorium for the prerace technical meeting. The room was filled with about three hundred runners who had earned the right to compete in the Olympic Trials. I don't think I have ever felt so much tension in a room. It was palpable. Yet I felt as if I were observing this tension from the clouds. I could feel it, but I wasn't in it. I was full of God's peace and presence.

When I was warming up for the race, I was so relaxed that I nearly missed the start. I decided to visit the portapotty one last time, and when I came out, all I saw was the women warming up. When I looked down the road, I saw all the men lined up on the starting line. I quickly did one last stride, arriving at the start with about ten seconds to spare. I say all this to emphasize how being connected to God brings freedom, relaxation, and joy, allowing one to perform at new levels. (Just make sure you don't miss the start of your race!)

When the gun fired, I went straight to the front. Houston's course was flat and fast, so I was eager to make it a fast race from the start, rather than the slow races that Olympic Trials tend to be because everyone is not wanting to lead. We were out aggressively and on pace to run very fast through the first ten miles, despite its being a windy day. The lead pack gradually dwindled until it was down to half a dozen or so guys at the halfway mark. I was still experiencing the presence of God and feeling like I was more in church than at the Olympic Trials. It was incredible.

Then something shifted. Instead of focusing on being connected to God, I got distracted by the wind. It's a little embarrassing to admit that something as small as the wind could alter my connection with God, but sometimes it's the small things that disrupt our spirits, because often our guard isn't up with the small things. I became frustrated that I was having to lead almost the entire race, breaking the wind for everyone behind me. My frustration wasn't justified, though. I had the freedom to choose my race strategy, and I was choosing to lead and to run hard. But that frustration began to grow.

A few miles later, I was weaving across the road like a racecar before the start of a NASCAR race, trying to get someone to help me with the pace. From that moment on, my connection with God was broken as my focus shifted away from Him to the wind, and my body quickly started feeling the consequences. When we came through with one lap to go (about six miles), only three of us remained in the lead group. We all knew that if we worked together, we all would make the Olympic team. Abdi Abdirahman, one of the three, fell back a few miles later, leaving Meb Keflezighi and me alone at the front. At about mile twenty-four, I hit the dreaded "wall." All of my marathons had been hard, but I could always dig deep and push myself to the finish. Hitting the wall, though, is different from running through the usual pain. I felt like I was having an out-of-body experience, and I felt unable to push. It was humbling. I believe this fatigue was a result of my glycogen stores becoming depleted from not finishing the Cytomax sports drink I always took every 5K of a marathon. Because I had been taking ibuprofen to help ease the pain in my plantar, my stomach got more and more flared up as the race went on. I had taken my first few bottles of Cytomax without any problems, but then I got really bad acid reflux and felt like I would vomit up any liquid I tried to take in. As the race wore on, I tried to force down as much Cytomax as I could, but I wasn't getting much at all, so it was no surprise that I started feeling out of it. I remember saying a prayer at that point, one that I imagine almost every marathoner has prayed at this stage in the race: "Lord, help me get there." I didn't know how I was going to cover the next two miles in my depleted state, but I knew I needed to reconnect with God if I was going to make it.

As I reconnected with God through prayer, I felt grace for every step. It wasn't my fastest two miles ever, but I was able to hold on to my second-place position and qualify for my second Olympic team. Reflecting on that Olympic Trials, I can't help but wonder how the race might have played out had I not gotten frustrated by the wind and instead kept my connection with God the whole race. I'm not saying I would have won, but I think it would have been a much different, more enjoyable experience had I stayed connected in worship.

What I learned that day is how important it is for me to guard my connection with God. The Bible says that the devil is always on the prowl, looking for someone to devour (1 Peter 5:8). While I don't like being overly focused on the devil, I have learned to be aware that we have an adversary who is the "father of lies" (John 8:44). For this reason, I don't know whether every lie that comes into my head is *from* the devil, but I do know that it is *of* the devil, because of his identity as the father of lies. And we need to identify these lies so we can combat them with the Word of God. The lie I believed that day was that it wasn't fair for me to be doing all of the work on a windy day. Yet that simply wasn't true. I had chosen to run at the front, and it wasn't anyone's responsibility to help me. Believing that lie, though, led to frustration, and that frustration led to my body getting tense and tight, which kept it from operating at its maximal potential.

Being in a state of worship and connection with God is incredibly empowering, yet it can also feel nebulous at times, leaving me thinking, *What does it really mean to worship God through running?* Pondering this thought, I've realized that worshiping God through anything is simple, really—it's just doing whatever you are doing with the heart posture that it is for Him. Getting to this point at the 2012 Olympic Marathon Trials was built through worship, the encouraging words of others, and learning to see God as He sees me. Once we get to that state of connection with God and can feel our worship pour out in the process of doing our craft, let us hold tightly to this posture, for it can easily slip, as it did for me with the wind. I needed this lesson, because after this race I was confronted by distractions and lies that threatened to take my focus from running for, to, and unto God.

Some of the moments when I entered this state of worship while running the strongest happened when no one else but God was there. I can still remember one run when I was out in the forest all by myself hearing nothing but the wind through the trees and the quiet patter of my feet on the dirt trail, floating effortlessly, having my heart, mind, and body set on Him in a deep state of worship. It gave me the chills then and it still does now as I remember it. These moments, unlike winning an Olympic gold medal, are available to all of us, and they are even more valuable.

Declaration

"I'll have locker number 204," I would say every day while checking in to the gym near my home in Mammoth Lakes. At this point in my career, I had already run 2:06:17 for the marathon but was dreaming of one day running 2:04. I had been learning from the Bible and my mentors of faith that there is power in our words. I was inspired by passages such as James 3:5: "So also the tongue is a small part of the body, and yet it boasts of great things. See how great a forest is set aflame by such a small fire!" And:

- "Truly I say to you, whoever says to this mountain, 'Be taken up and cast into the sea,' and does not doubt in his heart, but believes that what he says is going to happen, it will be granted him" (Mark 11:23).
- "He said to me, 'Son of man, can these bones live?' And I answered, 'O Lord GOD, You know.' Again He said to me, 'Prophesy over these bones and say to them, "O dry bones, hear the word of the LORD." Thus says the Lord GOD to these bones, "Behold, I will cause breath to enter you that you may come to life. I will put sinews on you,

make flesh grow back on you, cover you with skin and put breath in you that you may come alive; and you will know that I am the LORD"'" (Ezek. 37:3–6).

These passages inspired me to cultivate a daily practice of declaring my heart's dream that I would one day run a 2:04 marathon. It wasn't that I was walking around telling everyone who would listen about this goal; I made these declarations in private (like when I was out doing my afternoon runs on my own), perhaps to Sara and a few other close friends, and in sneaky ways that maybe no one else would pick up on, like asking for locker 204.

Fast-forward to the fall of 2010, when I was training in Mammoth Lakes for the Chicago Marathon. I was running the marathon for the charity that Sara and I had founded the year before, the Hall Steps Foundation, so I decided to take the shoes I planned to race in and have all the other runners on our charity team for Chicago sign them in an act of solidarity. I also signed the shoes, writing "2:04 for the poor" as another form of declaration and because the funds raised would go to our projects helping impoverished communities in both Chicago and Kenya. Unfortunately, my declaration didn't come to pass that fall. I struggled with fatigue and didn't make it to the starting line of the Chicago Marathon. But I saved those shoes for my next marathon, which happened to be the 2011 Boston Marathon. I remember looking at the shoes before the race and thinking that "2:04 for the poor" was not likely to happen on such a challenging course. One of the hardest courses in the professional circuit, the race had been run for 113 years and no one had ever run faster than 2:05:52.

Later that week I found myself on the starting line in Hopkinton with the flag blowing in the direction we would be running on our 26.2-mile journey into downtown Boston. As I mentioned earlier, a tailwind on marathon day was a rare occurrence, and I knew I had to make the most of it. When the gun fired, I went straight to the front, determined not to allow one mile to pass without attacking it. I remember at one point in the race feeling the wind at my back and looking up into the blue sky and smiling at God. It was as if He was pushing us along, an amazing sensation I will never forget.

We hit the halfway point at 61:56, well under world record pace and a time that would end up being the third fastest half marathon of my life. I hung with the leaders until mile twenty, when three runners surged, breaking away from the lead pack. I ended up finishing fourth in 2:04:58, more than thirty seconds under the American record. Even though my time was wind aided and not legal for record purposes because it was a point-to-point course, it was every bit as satisfying as an American record because it fulfilled what I had been declaring for years. I still have those shoes in my garage, and every once in a while I'll pick them up and smile when I look at the faded words "2:04 for the poor," because I felt that race was declared into existence much in the same way that Ezekiel declared to the dry bones to come to life. This experience continues to remind me not to put time limits on the dreams I'm believing will happen. I easily could have stopped declaring I was going to run 2:04 after failing the first time, but I would have missed that declaration's fulfillment.

To some, the concept of declarations may seem eerily similar to a popular book called *The Secret*, whose premise is that you can get whatever you want in life if you just envision it and wish for it. Though I do not believe that to be totally true, I think there is some truth to the power of declarations. From the beginning of the Bible, God creates the whole world by speaking everything into existence (Gen. 1:3, 6, 9, 14, 20, 24, 26). If I am made in God's image and likeness, having His powerful Spirit inside me, so too am I able to speak with declarations and create life in any hopeless situation.

Today, one of my favorite ways to practice declarations with my kids is to use their negative declarations in the opposing form. For example, often I'll be in the car driving my daughters around and chatting with them about their day, and they will open up about something they are struggling with and end their assessment by saying, "I'm just not good at it." As soon as I hear a negative "I am" statement, that's my trigger to help my kids (or me) make an opposing positive declaration. So if they say, "I'm not smart," I have them say with me, "I am smart." It's really that simple. It feels a little awkward and they might not want to do it at first (especially if they are teenagers), but it's powerful in reversing their negative declaration, and I almost always see a difference in their attitude. My pastor, Eric Johnson, taught me that instead of saying, "I'm not good at . . ." you can say, "I am currently struggling with . . ." This is a much healthier way to verbalize a struggle without making it a character flaw that, if we believe it, will only perpetuate in our lives.

The words we say are powerful, so find ways to declare positive things over yourself and others every day. Perhaps the most powerful times we can make these declarations are in moments of weakness. Someone ought to put up a giant sign at the twenty-mile mark (the point in the race traditionally known as "the wall") of every marathon that declares, "Let the weak say I am strong." I can just imagine watching runners run through their wall as they declare over and over, "I am strong." But let us not just declare in our weakness; let us also declare the deepest dreams in our hearts and speak life into every area that seems hopeless.

Fearless

"Be bold" were Sara's last words to me before I took to
the track in the 5,000-meters at the US National Track and
Field Championships in 2005. It was just weeks after I had
finished my collegiate career at Stanford, and I was competing against the best professional athletes in the nation. I
had never made a world championship team—or even been
close to qualifying for one—but I was coming off a collegiate
national championship at that distance just a few weeks prior
at NCAAs.

Sara's advice to "be bold" comes from Joshua 1:6–7, which
says, "Be strong and courageous, for you shall give this people
possession of the land which I swore to their fathers to give
them. Only be strong and very courageous; be careful to do
according to all the law which Moses My servant commanded
you; do not turn from it to the right or to the left, so that you
may have success wherever you go."

This advice was exactly what I needed to hear before the
race. When the gun fired, the top-seeded runner, Tim Broe,
took off and quickly opened up a gap on everyone else. It was
clear that Tim wanted to run fast, but no one else was willing
to go with him. Our chase group stayed about twenty meters
back for the first couple of laps until Sara's words popped into

my mind: "Be bold." I accelerated hard, and my teammate Ian Dobson also went with me. We were able to catch up to Tim and work together to maintain the gap over the chase group, which earned all three of us spots on the world championship team. That race ended up being the fastest 5,000 meters I would ever run (13:16, finishing third), but it never would have happened had I not taken the advice to be bold.

Looking back at my career, I think it was my fearlessness that set me apart as a runner. In a time when runners of European descent were usually afraid to mix it up with the East Africans who were dominating the marathon, I wasn't afraid to run with the best guys in the world for a number of reasons, one of which was that I was okay with failure. After God helped me sort out how I saw myself—back when I took a break from Stanford during my sophomore year—I felt freed to take big risks, because my performances no longer defined my worth. I realized that my worth came from how God saw me, not from how I performed. Coupled with having a secure identity was the vision God had given me for my running. Strong vision plus a secure identity allows you to risk everything without the fear of failure. It's a potent combination.

Now, I do need to say that taking risks didn't always mean success for me. Sometimes taking a risk resulted in my blowing up and failing miserably. But one thing I know for sure, not one of the best performances of my career would have happened had I not taken a big risk.

In 2006, I was experimenting with longer races. I ran my first race longer than 12K at the USATF 20K Championships in New Haven, and then a few months later ran another at the World Road Running Championships in Debrecen, Hungary. Both of those 20Ks went well—I earned a national title in the first race and finished eleventh at the World Championships in a new American record. I continued to move up in distances and eventually began training for my first marathon. I loved the challenge of running longer than I'd ever run before. I would lie in bed at night and feel my calves throbbing from the extra miles—and I loved the sensation. My body was responding better to training than it had ever responded before, perhaps because I was introducing a new stimulus. I was getting fitter with each week.

My coach, Terrence Mahon, and I decided that I would run my first ever half marathon in Houston in January of 2007. We agreed that if the half went well, I would debut in the marathon later that spring in Los Angeles. At that time, my training was geared more toward the marathon than the half marathon, so I didn't taper a whole lot prior to Houston. Despite that, my legs felt the best they had ever felt—or would ever feel in my entire career. Sara and I drove from Mammoth Lakes to my hometown to spend a few nights in Big Bear before heading to Houston. Unfortunately, the night before we left for Houston, Big Bear got hit by a massive snowstorm. I went for a run in about a foot of fresh powder the morning we were supposed to leave, a mere two days before the race. Running in snow usually left me feeling sluggish and heavy legged, yet even with my feet sinking with each step, my legs felt light and bouncy. I was amazed! I knew something special could happen in Houston, but first I had to get there.

I put chains on our tires before we left Big Bear and started the treacherous, windy drive on icy roads down the mountain to the Ontario airport. We didn't make it far before we found ourselves sliding out of control into a ditch. I'd been nervous that the slow drive was going to make us miss our flight, so my stress level was already high. When we slid off the road, I punched the steering wheel as hard as I could in frustration—not exactly the calm and collected version of myself I was hoping to be before the race. Luckily, someone stopped and towed us out of the ditch and we were on our way again. We drove a few more miles before getting to the CHP officer, who informed us that all roads out of Big Bear had been closed. At this point, my stress consumed me. I wasn't sure I'd make the race at all, and I figured that even if I did, my race would be shot thanks to the stress.

I called my agent and we rebooked our flight for the following day. Traveling the day before the race wasn't our normal practice, and it isn't ideal for racing, but it was our only choice. We waited out the storm for a few hours at a little roadside diner halfway down the mountain until the roads had been cleared enough to reopen, and I tried to gather myself emotionally.

I finally arrived in Houston the next day with just enough daylight remaining to drive the course with my coach and then eat a pasta dinner. I wasn't able to sleep well that night, not because I was nervous but because I had a terrible headache. Sara massaged my temples and hands to relieve the pain, and eventually I dozed for a few hours. This might have been the worst lead-up to a race I'd had in my career. I'd like to say that during the night I had an encounter with God and He melted the stress away and gave me peace in the storm, but that wouldn't necessarily be true. What I was feeling, more than anything, was that something big was about to happen and that God was protecting me from the enemy, who was trying to stop it. It felt like I was in the middle of a war but not being wounded by the enemy's weapons.

The morning of the race, I used a ballpoint pen to write two potential pace charts on my hand, with each chart telling me what time I needed to cross each mile of the race to run a given race time. My coach and I figured that if I had an "A" day, I could get under the American record (Mark Curp's twenty-two-year-old time of 60:55), requiring me to run 4:37 per mile. In theory, I wasn't supposed to go out faster than a 4:37 pace. There was also a slower pace chart in case I was having a "B" day, which would be around 4:40 per mile, a solid debut time for the half marathon, but not an American record.

When the race started, I went straight to the front and found a comfortable rhythm. This was prior to the era of GPS watches, so I had no idea how fast I was running. I just tried to picture myself in training, running at a level of effort I felt I could sustain for an hour. People often ask me how to find the proper pace to race. I found that when I was training, I would visualize myself in the race to prepare my mind for what I wanted to do, but when I was in the actual race, I visualized being in practice. This may seem odd, but my reasoning was that I needed to be able to determine what level of effort I could maintain for each distance. During the race, when I was fresh from tapering my training and adrenaline was kicking in, rather than rely on my watch to tell me what pace I should run, I could go into my mind's eye and ask, "If I were running this effort in practice, could I maintain it for this race distance?" I found this to be the best way to find the right pace because sometimes things are clicking and you don't want your watch or your mind to hold you back. Conversely, sometimes things aren't clicking and you shouldn't be running as fast as you think you should be.

My first mile at Houston was 4:37, right on pace for an A day, but it felt too easy. Despite being all alone at the front and not needing to run any faster, I decided to risk putting my foot on the gas a little more. I was surprised when I reached the two-mile mark and saw that my pace had gotten significantly faster, down to a 4:32 mile. At that point, I could have gotten either excited that I was well ahead of schedule or fearful that I was going to blow up because I'd gone out too hard. Usually, the advice for running a half or full marathon is "don't go out too hard," so fear can be a natural reaction when your splits are ahead of schedule. But I always remember Jim Ryun saying that when he arrived at the end of a lap of a mile race and his pace was faster than scheduled, he chose to see being ahead of schedule as a positive. So I decided to be excited rather than fearful, and when I got excited, I picked up the pace without realizing it. When I arrived at the third mile, I checked my watch and was even more surprised to see 4:28, a pace I had not even imagined running.

Looking back at the Houston Half Marathon, I still don't fully understand how it happened. There is no way—especially considering the crazy travel and stress I endured the few days before the race and the fact that I was in the middle of a hard block of marathon training, which should have left my legs feeling fatigued—that I should have been running as fast as I was. I led the race from start to finish, and the only real trouble I had was at mile ten, when my stomach turned and I wondered if it was going to cause problems. I immediately started praying, and shortly thereafter the pain was gone.

Many athletes reflect on their greatest performances and comment, "It was the easiest race I ever ran." I would echo that, because I never felt like I had to dig deep, push harder than ever before, or endure more pain than I was previously able. It was the most enjoyable and least painful race I ever ran. I didn't hit the wall in those last few miles. I felt like I wanted to run another half marathon. I'm still curious what my marathon time would have been had I kept going. Once I was close enough to the finishing line to see the clock read

59:43, I pumped my fist in excitement and let out a yell—very uncharacteristic of me, but I couldn't contain myself. That moment was a dream come true—running not just the best time ever by an American but also a time competitive with the best guys in the world. And the best part of the race for me was that my parents, wife, and coach got to ride in the lead vehicle and watch the race unfold. They were able to partake in my greatest performance, which felt so right, because they had been with me on a journey that never would have happened without them. It also wouldn't have happened had I let the fear of going out faster than expected trump the boldness of taking a big risk.

Playing it conservatively isn't the opposite of risk. Fear is. Only if we can live without fear can we perform at our very best. Fear has always made me feel heavy and tight. Whenever I was running out of fear, I felt locked up, and nothing good ever came from it. I knew I needed to overcome fear, and I did it by discovering who I was and learning where my value came from apart from running.

It also helped me to live out my greatest fear. I can't tell you how many races I'd had in the eleven years before the Houston Half Marathon in which I blew up and ran terribly. But it was living out those failures that made me realize I could live through them and be okay. Sometimes the worst part of failing is anticipating how bad it's going to feel. But when you live it out, you end up thinking, "Hey, that wasn't that bad." This is another reason experiencing failure can be so important—it breaks the fear associated with it. Throughout my career, I would be on the starting line repeating the words "be bold" under my breath as I waited for the gun. I'm so glad that running boldly became part of who I was, because I never would have discovered my potential without it.

Love

Eight years after I set the American half marathon record in Houston, Sara and I decided to start a family through the process of adoption. I could write an entire book on what the adoption process was like for us, but let me just say that growing up, I never intended to adopt—not because I was opposed to the idea but simply because I lacked exposure to adoptive families. Sara, however, had grown up with adopted kids in her extended family, and from a young age said she would adopt kids.

On our first date, Sara told me that when she was a little girl, she drew a picture of herself and her adopted kids, a dream she had for her life. I, on the other hand, knew what adoption was, of course, but hadn't ever thought about it for my future family. But God began to work on me, showing me how beautiful adoption is. And I now believe there is no better way to experience God's heart toward us. After all, we are the adopted children of God: "But when the fullness of the time came, God sent forth His Son, born of a woman, born under the Law, so that He might redeem those who were under the law, that we might receive the adoption as sons.

Because you are sons, God has sent forth the Spirit of His Son into our hearts, crying, 'Abba! Father!' Therefore you are no longer a slave, but a son; and if a son, then an heir through God" (Gal. 4:4–7).

When we started our family's adoption process, we were number seventy-eight on a waiting list to adopt a baby from Ethiopia under the age of two. Since we didn't have children, we thought it would be good to start as close to "day one" as possible. Sara and I had been to Ethiopia a number of times, spending months training in the thin air at nine thousand feet just outside of Addis Ababa, and we had fallen in love with the country, people, and culture. Also, our hearts broke for the six million orphans, some of whom we saw working as shoe shiners and living on the streets of Addis. I remember in one instance, a street kid who couldn't have been more than ten years old asked me if he could shine my running shoes. My heart broke for him as I noticed his tattered clothing. I said *ishi* ("okay" in Amharic) and asked how much it would cost. He told me it would be five birr, the equivalent of twenty-five cents in US dollars. The boy worked hard on my shoes for ten minutes, taking his low-wage job seriously, shining my running shoes in a flurry of brushing strokes. He finished one shoe, showing it to me proudly as he compared it with my other shoe, which had not yet been shined. He beamed as if to say, "Look what I just did!" I tried to act amazed too, which was difficult because my heart was so sad for him, and I replied *gobez* (Amharic for "wonderful"). When he finished, I gave him the equivalent of five dollars—which I don't normally do, because I am aware of how foreigners can negatively impact the local economy when they give, but sometimes the Holy Spirit leads me to give, as was the case here. You should have seen the boy's face light up! You would have thought he had just won the lottery. He ran off with all his friends like it was the best day of his life. Moments like these put into perspective how blessed I am to have more than enough and at the same time make me determined to find a sustainable way to assist people in situations similar to his.

During the time we were on the waiting list, we visited our adoption agency's orphanage in Addis, where we were surprised to discover that many older kids in the orphanage were waiting for families to adopt them. This struck me as odd. While we were waiting for our child, there were children waiting for families. After meeting and interacting with the kids in the orphanage, the thought passed through my mind that I would take any one of them home in an instant. I don't know about you, but something shifts in my heart when I go from hearing about a problem to actually seeing and being confronted with it. In this scenario, the problem wasn't the orphanage—the orphanage was a nice facility with an excellent staff that was taking good care of the children who lived there. Yet it bothered me to see kids growing up in an orphanage, because orphanages clearly aren't God's ideal for kids—families are. I couldn't help but imagine what my childhood and my life would have been like if I'd grown up without a family. Sara had had a similar experience that day in the orphanage, so when we finished our training stint in Ethiopia, we went home and changed all of our agency paperwork to allow us to adopt a waiting older child.

Not long after that, we became aware of "Four Girls" (which is how they referred to themselves when they were picking up the English language, as if they were legendary, and that phrase has stuck in our family) just before Christmas 2014. Sara was part of an adoption group on Facebook, where there was a post circulating that four biological sisters in

Ethiopia had been waiting for a family for more than three years. The adoption agency in charge of their placement was discussing breaking them up into pairs and having them adopted by two different families, which really bothered me. I'm in the middle of five kids and can't imagine being separated from any of my siblings, especially if unfortunate circumstances had already separated us from our parents. I thought, *I can't let this happen.*

As I weighed what to do, I felt much the way I did in a race before I hit the front of the pack. Usually the only thing holding me back from going out too fast and leading was the fear of failure. Yet as I learned throughout my career, and through my time spent with God, I should never let fear hold me back from where God is leading me. As 2 Timothy 1:7 says, "For God has not given us a spirit of fear and timidity, but of power, love, and self-discipline" (NLT). Nevertheless, it was a weighty decision. We had spoken to many families who had adopted older kids from Ethiopia, and they had walked a very hard road. These kids had all come out of trauma and at times even had difficulty connecting emotionally with their new families. Adoption is basically signing your name on a blank contract not knowing what you will face but deciding that come what may, you will be loving and taking care of these kids for the rest of your life.

Instead of being led by fear, I've tried to make decisions motivated by love. What has God put love in my heart to do? If I love to run hard and go to the front and push the pace, then I should do that because that's how God created me. Much in the same way, if God had given me love in my heart for these four girls, I should follow that love, not the feelings of inadequacy that often accompany taking a big risk. Sara and I decided to change our paperwork yet again, and this time we even had to change agencies because the Four Girls weren't being represented by our agency, which meant we had to forfeit the large fees we had already paid and start the process all over. We could have viewed this as a big hassle, but it wasn't really that hard because we were motivated by love. This was the first lesson God taught me during the adoptive process: He pursues me, and He is willing to pay a high price to bring me into His family. I felt God's heart toward me as I whipped through stacks of paperwork and wrote checks to adopt our girls. As I did this, I often thought to myself that God loved me even more than the love I was feeling toward my girls, which blew my mind.

We did run into some problems along the way, which isn't unusual for adoption, especially international adoption. Apparently, our social worker in the States didn't believe in us as much as we believed in ourselves, because she refused to approve us to adopt the girls. She said she would approve us for two of the girls, but because we were relatively young (thirty-two years old) and had never had kids, she didn't feel we were ready for the challenge. We, however, chose to believe God rather than believe her, and we knew God would give us the grace for the challenging road ahead, so we switched social workers. Our second social worker didn't see her job as telling us whether we were up for the challenge but rather making sure we had a safe home and the means to provide well (financially, emotionally, etc.) for our kids. She approved us without hesitation, and the ball began to roll.

One thing I've learned from racing is that when you go to the front and push the pace, the worst thing you can do is second-guess yourself and slow down. I always experienced moments at the front when I doubted myself, wondering, *Did I go out too hard? Am I running too fast? Can I sustain this pace?* I found that whenever I believed that maybe I couldn't do this, I was always right. Whatever I doubted, I partnered with, and that partnership became a reality. I had to work hard not to partner with my doubts and instead to partner with God's truth that I am an overcomer. It was the same way with our adoption journey. There were times when seeds of doubt entered my mind, and I had to decide whether I was going to partner with those doubts or with God's truth. I knew that agreeing with God's truth always brings peace, joy, life, and satisfaction, but I still had to choose.

As the process continued, one thing became very important for me to do with the girls before we adopted them: give them a choice. I'm not going to get into the girls' story, because that is theirs to tell, but as you can imagine, they had been through a lot, none of which had been their choice. Things had just happened to them, and they were forced simply to react to those events. But I wanted the girls to choose us in much the same way that we chose them. In our relationship with God, He values our free will so much that He was willing to risk it all in the garden of Eden so that we could have a choice. The risk He took cost the life of His Son, Jesus, who was crucified as a result of our poor choices, which alienated us from God. This shows how much God values free will, and He values it because that's what true relationships are built on—two people choosing each other.

After Sara and I had first become aware of the Four Girls and their urgent need to find a family, we told our agency that we would most likely adopt the girls but first wanted to come to Ethiopia and spend some time getting to know them and all the other kids in the orphanage (so that they didn't know why we were there) to get further clarification from God that this is what He was leading us to do. We booked last-minute tickets to travel halfway around the world and daily visited the orphanage to play and interact with all the kids, all the while keeping an eye on these four sisters. When we met the girls, there wasn't any voice or any light from heaven shining down on them, but we felt a growing love in our hearts. After about a week of spending time with them in the orphanage, we decided to ask them if they wanted to join our family.

I'll never forget the day we invited the girls into our family. The nurse at the orphanage called them into her small office as she translated for us. (We knew a little Amharic, but not enough to communicate on a deep level.) When the nurse asked the girls if they wanted to join our family, they instantly started screaming, crying, and jumping up and down in joy, relieved of the burden of an unknown future. Their reaction answered our question, and our family of six was birthed. That moment was one of the most joy-filled moments of my life, one I will never forget. And it all happened because Sara and I decided to follow love instead of fear and take a risk.

Today, the girls are thriving. It has been so fun to see them grow and flourish in our home and society. Their ages, as of the writing of this book, are eighteen (Hana), fifteen (Mia), eleven (Jasmine), and eight (Lily). They are getting caught up academically (they never attended school in Ethiopia), are playing sports, are deeply spiritual, and are living a fairly normal American life. I say "fairly" normal because Sara and I place high value on living an adventurous life and sharing it with our kids, so we frequently travel together to races or on vacation and go back to Ethiopia often.

I often find myself commenting on how amazing my kids are. I could write story after story with the opening line, "This definitely isn't normal kid behavior," but I'll give you just one example. We had just finished sitting on an airplane for twenty hours returning home from Ethiopia on our second visit back there since their adoption, and we had picked up our car and started the more than eight-hour trek from Los Angeles to our home in Redding. You would think the kids would be basket cases at the end of such an epic trip, but when we started the drive home, one of the girls said, "Dad, I want to give you an encouraging word," and she began to encourage me. Then the rest of the girls chimed in with their own uplifting words. This was just one of many moments I've experienced when you do something to bless others, only to realize that you are the one who has walked away with the biggest blessing. We are so blessed to have the Four Girls as our daughters!

When I was competing, one of my favorite things about being on the starting line was that it felt like a blank slate. Anything was possible at that moment, and even if I was coming off my worst race ever, it didn't necessarily mean I was going to race poorly that day. Running, like living fearlessly, should always be fun. I love taking risks. And I love it even more when taking risks pays off. I'm even learning to love the lesson I learn when the risk doesn't pay off.

When I was in high school and feeling the nerves before a big race, my dad (who was also my coach) used to tell me, "We leave outcomes up to God." Those words always comforted me because there is so much in running and in life that we don't have control over—results being one of those things—but we do have control over how we run, how we live, and what we are going to follow: love or fear. I would argue, from my experiences, that you never lose when you follow love, whether it be the way you run or choosing how you are going to build your family, because, as the Bible says, "Love never fails" (1 Cor. 13:8).

Partnering

My least favorite aspect of running is probably one that all runners can relate to: injuries. I was blessed throughout my high school days not to experience any serious injuries that required extended time off. Then, the summer before leaving for Stanford, I contracted tightness in my IT band (the tendon running on the outside of your thigh going from the hip to knee) that persisted through cross-country season. Once that cleared up, it was followed by chronic shin splints that lasted the rest of my freshman year. The first time I had a problem with my upper hamstring was in the summer before my sophomore year. I was home from Stanford for the summer and training very hard. I would run twice a day, spend an hour doing a *Yoga for Athletes* DVD, kick on a kickboard in the lake for twenty minutes for recovery, nap for an hour every afternoon, do self-massage with a foam roller and a softball, stretch, and also do some form of weight training and plyometric exercises. I couldn't think of anything else I could add to my training regimen. My entire day was consumed by becoming a better runner. I wanted to reach the vision God had given me, which meant leaving no stone unturned. But I wrongly assumed that hard work always yields better results, and it wasn't long before I developed a sharp pain in my upper hamstring where the muscle attaches to the bone.

I tried taking a couple of days off, but to no avail. I did some prone planking that seemed to strengthen the area where I was feeling pain. It hurt like crazy when I did the strengthening, but I had to try something. A few weeks later, the pain gave way and I was able to resume training, but the upper hamstring issue wasn't gone for good. Many of the injuries and fatigue issues I battled throughout my career were because I wasn't good at partnering with my body. I had the wrong mindset of believing that my body and my mind were functioning in opposition to each other, which is common reasoning in the endurance community. But over the years, I've learned that my body, mind, and spirit are all on the same team, wanting to operate as a unit to accomplish a common goal. When I started viewing my body as being on my side, I found that I was able to truly listen to my body and get much better results.

Fast-forward eight years to the 2012 London Olympic Marathon. Standing on the starting line, I knew my training hadn't gone ideally, but the plantar fasciitis I'd been battling for seven months had finally subsided. I was running in my first Olympics with God as my coach, and in my training I'd experienced a turning point in my running where I felt God was leading me to take the GPS (which tells me how fast I'm running) off my watch. I felt He was telling me to reconnect with my body and run the right effort for my workouts rather than run the right pace. I still remind Sara of this now that I coach her. When she asks what pace she should run a given workout or race, I reply, "The right pace," meaning find the pace your body is telling you it can handle for the distance, heightening the connection between your body and mind, rather than be married to a pace. Often we guess what the right pace should be for a workout or a race based on what times we have run in workouts, when really our bodies are able to run a lot faster than we think. I find it interesting that the most dominant runners in the world come from countries that are not as technologically advanced as we are in the West. Not being married to lots of gadgets allows them to run based on effort and not so much by pace. They are in tune with their bodies. Don't get me wrong, I'm not against using goal paces in training to get the body used to running at a certain speed, but we also have to understand that our bodies always know what pace we can handle for a given distance. The best way to run is by listening to the body, staying in tune with what it is communicating to the mind.

When I felt God leading me to stop looking at the pace of my workouts, I wasn't thrilled. I always thrived on trying to hit goal times in practice—and I do think there is a time and a place for that—and the thought of doing a fifteen-mile hard run and not knowing how fast I was going didn't seem very rewarding. But my body was on such a downward spiral that I wasn't able to finish my workouts anyway because the pace I was trying to run was too aggressive for what my body was capable of. I felt like I was beating my head against a wall trying to force my body to do something it didn't want to do, so I had to try something, and this is what I felt God's answer was—taking the GPS off my watch.

It felt strange to look down at my running watch and not see a pace. It annoyed me at first, but I quickly learned that when I ran according to how my body felt rather than according to pace, I was able to finish my workouts. This was a step in the right direction, so I kept at it. For the last few months before the Olympics, I never knew what pace I was running for any of my workouts, which made me a little nervous because I usually knew exactly what kind of shape I was in based on my workout times. But deciding to partner with my body helped me make it to the starting line in better mental and emotional states than if I had been discouraged by not hitting workout times and not finishing workouts. Sometimes our biggest victories aren't the races we win. Sometimes they're the personal battles we win along the way.

Regardless of my training, when I was standing on the starting line of the Olympic Marathon, I felt the same optimism I'd felt in all of my marathons—like anything was possible. Considering how shaky my training had been, it was probably good for me not to know how fast I'd been running those last couple of months. It kept me in suspense. I told myself that maybe I was running faster than I'd ever run before. The mystery of not knowing exactly what speed I'd been running gave me confidence, which was the opposite of gaining confidence by performing certain workouts at a certain pace. I've always believed that with God, all things are possible. When I was in high school, I chose Luke 1:37—"For nothing will be impossible with God"—to put on the back of my warmups. So I truly believed that perhaps that day would be my biggest breakthrough and my best race ever. They even played the *Chariots of Fire* theme song as I warmed up near the starting line, which is my favorite movie. Come on! What better sign could I have gotten?

The gun fired and we were off. The course weaved around the city of London on small, narrow roads packed with more fans than I'd ever seen on a marathon course. The atmosphere was electric, and I was relishing it. I felt like I was running in a Tour de France stage, with people right on top of us yelling so loudly that it was hard to hear yourself think. Unfortunately, the electric atmosphere didn't carry into how my body was feeling. I found myself fading within the first 10K of the race. The pace just felt too hard. But that was okay—I had lost contact with the leaders in major marathons and been able to catch up, and I knew how to encourage myself through it, so I kept telling myself I'd start feeling better soon and catch up to the leaders. When the going gets tough in a race, positive self-talk is usually the only thing that can turn the tables. Whatever I think, I begin to believe, and whatever I believe, I live out. I kept telling myself the simplest yet most encouraging mantra I could pull on: *You're doing great, you're doing great.* But sometimes no matter how much positive self-talk you use, your body doesn't respond and the truth becomes evident that you just aren't fit enough—it's that simple. I wonder how many times I've beaten myself up for not being mentally tough when actually I simply wasn't physically fit enough to run as fast as I wanted. To run an incredible race, it takes body, mind, and spirit firing on all cylinders. The mental side of running is important, but it isn't everything.

At about 10K, I felt the upper hamstring problem that I'd battled in college. Having experienced this sensation before, I thought I could work through it, but a few miles later, the pain had intensified and was quite sharp. The tricky thing about injuries is that there are some you can run through and some you can't. I always give the athletes I coach a rule of thumb: if the pain gets increasingly worse or feels sharp as you run, then it's best not to run through it. When my hamstring pain started to feel sharp, I asked God what I should do. If He wanted me to be the guy hobbling across the finishing line hours after the winner had come through, I would hobble through the next twenty miles, but if He wanted me to stop,

I would do it, even though I'd never dropped out of a race in my entire life. Whether it was refusing to walk during the school jog-a-thon or going out way too fast in a marathon and paying for it later, I always found what I needed to make it to the finishing line, but today things felt different, like I was going to cause real harm to my body, so for the first time ever I seriously considered dropping out.

In my conversation with God, I felt Him clearly communicate that I needed to partner with my body, and if I wasn't able to run 26.2 miles in a healthy manner, I needed to save my body to fight that battle on another day. Even though I felt I clearly heard this, I still needed to talk it over with Him. I couldn't imagine God telling me to throw in the towel, yet I also knew I could trust Him. If He was telling me to stop, it was in my best interest. What helped me step off the race course was when I heard God tell me, "It's better to lose with God than to win without Him." I had put all my trust in God to lead my training, and now to fail on the world's biggest stage felt all wrong, but that's because I didn't have the definition of success that God did. The truth was—and continues to be—that knowing God is the true victory we are all so hungry for.

I'm going to be honest with you. When I stepped off the race course, it felt wrong. It was a surreal moment for me. I kept thinking, *Is this really happening?* It felt so odd to stop running and start walking that I almost started running again. I struggle to share this story because it doesn't have a happy ending. I would like to say that I started listening to my body after that race, a decision that resulted in a tremendous physical breakthrough, but the truth is that didn't happen. My body continued to break down over the next four years as I struggled through injury after injury and eventually battled extreme fatigue. By January 2016 (prior to the Rio Olympic Trials), I sat down and took an honest look at the past four years. I finally faced the truth that the constant stream of injuries and fatigue were my body's way of telling me, "I've given you everything I could for twenty years—there is nothing left." I knew then that it was my time to hang up my shoes, and I retired a month before the 2016 Olympic Marathon Trials.

I also struggle to tell this story because it's easy for me to write about my breakthroughs and the things I did well, but it's not as much fun to share the lessons that did not result in victory. Just the other day I was sitting in church during worship, singing a song with a verse that says, "You teach my feet to dance upon disappointment." As I sang, I felt like God was telling me not only that my victories would help others be victorious but also that my disappointments would result in other breakthroughs. This was hugely healing for me to hear. As with any other character flaw (in this instance, my not listening to my body for so many years), it's easy to feel shame, which results in bottling that disappointment up and hiding it from the world when I really should be dancing over that disappointment, knowing that it will result in breakthroughs for others and perhaps a future breakthrough for myself.

It felt strange after retiring to stand on the side of the road and watch Sara compete in the 2016 Olympic Marathon Trials, knowing I was supposed to be out trying to make the Olympic team too. Sara, however, had had a different mentality throughout her running career. She would train as hard as anyone out there, but if her body was giving her signs that she needed to slow down or take a few days off, she listened to it. She would tweak the training plan based on how her body was feeling. Like bamboo, she would bend but not break.

Alternately I would stick to the training plan until my body broke. I believe this is why, at age thirty-five, she is still running and getting faster (she had personal bests of 69:27 in the half marathon and 2:26:20 in the marathon last year) and I had to retire at age thirty-three.

Learning to listen to my body is a continual process, even on the other side of my professional running career. I still tend to force my body to do something because I'm rigidly following a schedule or have some rules in my head about what I should do, whether it's a nutrition regime or my weightlifting program. The problem with this "living by the law" mentality is that it doesn't allow room for the Holy Spirit to invade and influence how I am living or training. Famed running coach Renato Canova's idea of having the training plan follow the athlete and not the athlete follow the training plan is something I really work hard to maintain, whether it be with the pro runners in my group or the runners I coach online. I see forcing my body as one of the biggest mistakes of my career, and I find that it's also a common problem for other runners. The problem is it is so easy to download a generic program (I have even produced some of these programs myself) and just follow it without ever tweaking it to suit your needs. I have to remember that the goal isn't to follow a plan as much as it is to follow the Holy Spirit, who is right in front of us and wants to lead us into our own promised land.

We need to consider the areas where we have strict rules in place and ask God if He wants to invade those areas with His guidance. I'm not convinced that all rules are bad, but God has taught me in my running journey that it's better to follow principles than rules. Principles give us the why behind the rules and allow room for individual implementation, whereas rules are so rigid that while they might work for a while, at some point they will cause us to break. For example, I may have heard the rule that you should run intervals on Tuesday, a tempo on Friday, and a long run on Sunday. The principle behind this is great. I love the flow of this week and really believe it yields good results, but what if you slept terribly on Thursday night and are feeling sick and run down? Should you still proceed with the tempo? The obvious answer is no. But I would have answered yes because I was so legalistic with my training plan. Alternatively, if I had followed the principle behind this rule, I could have done the same sequence of workouts but listened to my body's feedback and given myself an extra recovery day.

I don't allow myself to look back at my career and think, *If only I had done x, y, z differently, what could I have done?* I think that could lead to some depressing thoughts. But while the window for me to change in my professional running career has closed, I know that this is an area of my life I need to continue to work on. As I reflect on my experience at the 2012 London Olympics and see the positive fruits that learning to partner with my body yielded (even though it may have been seen as failure in the eyes of the world), it reminds me to keep following tried and true principles that have been passed down from generation to generation and to always look to the Holy Spirit to give me moment-by-moment guidance. It says in the Bible, "Your word is a lamp to my feet and a light to my path" (Ps. 119:105), and so I go through my day asking God to illuminate the way.

Victories

On April 21, 2014, I found myself on the now-familiar starting line in Hopkinton, Massachusetts, about to race toward the finishing line in Boston, but this year felt different from the other three times I had run the race. I'd been scheduled to run the 2013 Boston Marathon but was in the middle of my post-London Olympic injury cycle and had been forced to withdraw a month or so prior. I still attended the race that year, but only to meet other runners, take pictures, and sign autographs. The 2013 race was the day of Sara's birthday (April 15), so I hopped on a flight that morning to get home in time to celebrate. When my plane touched down in San Francisco, I turned on my phone and received text after text from concerned family and friends asking if I was okay. I opened Twitter to see what all the concern was about, and that was when I first saw the news of the two bombs that had exploded at the finishing line of the Boston Marathon. My heart started racing and I was in a state of disbelief and shock. I thought of all the runners I'd just met, along with my friends and the amazing staff who put on the Boston Marathon, who were experiencing the horror of that day, wondering whether any of them were near those bombs.

I still can't make sense of what happened that day in Boston. The stories of loss and of overcoming catastrophe were heartbreaking and inspiring. I remember shortly thereafter driving to the airport for a business trip and hearing President Obama on the radio giving an inspiring speech, saying that both Boston and America would overcome this act of terrorism and return to the streets of Boston in 2014 to show the world how hard we can run: "We carry on. We race. We strive. We build and we work and we love and we raise our kids to do the same. And we come together to celebrate life and to walk our cities and to cheer for our teams when the Sox, then Celtics, then Patriots or Bruins are champions again, to the chagrin of New York and Chicago fans. The crowds will gather and watch a parade go down Boylston Street. And this time next year on the third Monday in April, the world will return to this great American city to run harder than ever and to cheer even louder for the 118th Boston Marathon."

The president's inspiring words ignited a fire inside me for the following year's race. I was filled with the desire to run harder and better than ever. If America ever needed someone to win a marathon, it was now. I texted my friend and fellow professional marathoner Meb Keflezighi, who had also been scheduled to run the year of the bombing but had been forced to withdraw because of injury, telling him that we were going to fly next year. Meb texted back immediately, equally fired up for the race.

My preparations for the 2014 Boston Marathon were extensive and more demanding than ever, training in the thin air of Ethiopia alongside the world's best marathoners. If you have never tried to run at nine thousand feet elevation, I wouldn't recommend it, unless you like the sensation of running while trying to breathe through a straw. In the months leading up to the marathon, my training had finally taken a turn for the better, and I stayed healthy and was feeling as fit as I'd ever felt prior to a marathon. I had run twenty-three miles at approximately a 5:10 per mile average at a lower training location (about seven thousand feet) outside of Addis Ababa. I'd never been able to do this before in training, which led me to believe that perhaps something special awaited me in Boston. My weight was also lighter than it had ever been since high school, which I hoped was a sign of good fitness.

Now, I want to state something I learned about getting the most out of my body: lighter doesn't always equal faster. It's so easy to buy into the mentality that the lighter I get, the faster I can run. Many distance runners, myself included, believe this because, to a certain extent, it's true. As a marathon runner, you want to be carrying as little extra weight as possible. But not all weight is bad. For example, I ran all my best races at 137–139 pounds. I had times when I weighed more than this and ran okay but not great, and I also had times when I raced much lighter and ran terribly. The worst race of my entire running career was when I was far too light at five foot ten and 127 pounds. It's easy to look at the Kenyan and Ethiopian athletes and assume that to run like them, you need to look like them and weigh the same as they do. (When you look at the start list of all the best male African runners, they're usually all around 120 pounds.) But I didn't find this to be true. I found that the only time I was competitive with the African runners was when I was at the right weight for me. I felt strong at 137–139 pounds, not weak and run down. So while I was coming into the 2014 Boston Marathon noticeably leaner than usual, it gave me an extra shot of confidence, but in reality my body simply didn't have the strength it needed to perform optimally.

Today when I coach my athletes, I reinforce the idea that I want them healthy and strong more than I want them light. I will even ask them to gain weight if I feel they're too lean. What always worked well for me was putting on a significant amount of weight (ten pounds) after each marathon (two per year). It was strategic weight gain to some extent and also just a nice break from being so disciplined with my nutrition for six months. I had observed a lot of African runners who commented that they would put on weight after their season was over, and it seemed to work well for them. I also learned to view this extra weight as training weight that would make my body stronger because I was pulling along extra resistance on every run. Despite knowing the benefits of adding weight postseason (the biggest of which I see to be allowing the body's hormonal system to reset itself, because being overly lean can add stress to that system), I always hated myself for putting on the weight, because it wasn't muscle. But every time I had the self-control not to indulge in junk food during my two-week break, I always either ran poorly in my next marathon or ended up injured or fatigued to the point where I didn't make it to the start of the race. Fueling is such an important issue in running, yet often calories are seen as the enemy rather than the vehicle that is going to take us to our goals. The African mentality is much different. Sara and I laugh when we share meals with our African friends, because their plates are loaded with more carbs than we've ever eaten in one sitting. Contrast this with many Western athletes who seem to be afraid of carbs. But the Africans are the ones dominating our sport. The reason they are so small is because they have smaller frames. I'm always amazed by how narrow my Ethiopian daughters' shoulders are. The Africans are just smaller, so trying to be the same weight as them is unrealistic for those who don't share their body type.

Getting back to the story, on the long journey home from Ethiopia, I felt full of optimism and excitement, as did the entire country, anticipating what would arguably be the most historically significant (for the United States) marathon in history. I felt that the professional running community had an obligation to show the world how we respond to acts of terrorism.

Standing on the starting line of the 2014 Boston Marathon, every American was fired up to be there and ready to push harder than ever to get an American victory, which hadn't happened since Greg Meyer won the race in 1983 (when I was six months old). The gun fired and the race started out similarly to my three previous Boston Marathons. I went straight to the front and tried to hammer it. Only this time, when I stepped on the gas, it was as if someone had put a governor on my body set to a five-minute-mile pace, which is fast for the everyday runner, but not fast enough for a world-class marathoner. I managed to stay toward the front for six miles or so and was glad to have Meb's familiar face up front with me. I could always tell when Meb was feeling good, because he would go to the front and start pushing the pace, as he was today, sharing the lead with me.

About 10K into the race, we hit a bottle stop. (For professional runners, the race sets out tables and collects bottles from us to place on them so we can get whatever special fluids we typically take in training.) As often happens at bottle stops, some surging took place. Meb and another American opened up a small gap on the rest of the field. I found it odd that no one seemed concerned, not attempting to close the gap that Meb—the 2009 NYC Marathon champion and the Olympic silver medalist in the 2004 Athens Olympic Marathon—had opened up on us. The gap grew a little, but the leaders stayed within sight for quite some time.

I stayed at the front of the chase pack, trying to set a fast pace even though I wasn't feeling the usual spring in my step. I always stayed optimistic in races, though, because I knew that there were times when I would feel like trash but would come out on the other side feeling good again if I fought through those times. However, during the next couple of miles, I realized that how I was running didn't make any sense. Here I was, helping the rest of the mainly non-American field stay close to my friend and countryman when I knew that America badly needed something special to celebrate that day, like a win. I felt like I was on the same team as Meb in the Tour de France—he was in the break group, and I was in the chase group. But usually if a team puts a rider in the break group, they never lead in the chase group because they don't want to pull the chase group up to their rider late in the race. They want to give their man as much of a time gap as possible. Yet here I was leading the chase group. I also had the thought that if the tables were turned and I was in the breakaway group and Meb was in the chase group, how would I appreciate Meb running? I say "appreciate" because it isn't expected that just because we are Americans, we will sacrifice for a countryman. It's quite the opposite. Most Americans are afraid to take the lead because they know it will hurt their performance. Often, when there is no pacemaker, it makes for a slow, tactical, and—in my mind—boring race. If I'm watching the 1,500 meters in the Olympics, I want to see who the best runner in the world is for the 1,500 meters, not which 1,500-meter runner can run the fastest final 400 meters after jogging the first three laps. But I know not everyone shares my opinion and I'm okay with that.

Rethinking my race strategy, I knew that if I were in the lead group, I would appreciate Meb not leading the chase group and at least making the non-American runners work on their own to chase me down. I would want as much room to work with as possible, especially considering how remarkably early Meb made his move and how long he would have to push out there on his own. So I decided to simply treat someone else the way I would want to be treated. I veered to the side and relinquished the lead, and the pace of our chase group slowed drastically. It was as if no one knew what to do. But it wasn't long before another American in the chase group, tired of the dawdling pace, took the lead. When this happened, I ran next to that runner and proposed my race strategy to him. It was hard to explain while running so hard, barely able to breathe, but the other American runners eventually got the message and agreed to make the non-Americans work to chase Meb down, and I was grateful they were willing to adopt my mindset.

The gap between us and Meb opened to the point where he, along with the lead motorcycle, was out of sight, which is a big deal in marathoning. Once you're out of sight, you have a huge advantage. It's tremendously encouraging when you can see someone in front of you and notice the gap closing, but if you can't see them, you have no idea how big the gap is. We don't get earpieces feeding us information, like the riders do in the Tour de France. Instead, we have to rely on people on the side of the road yelling for us and telling us what is happening up ahead.

I don't remember when I fell off the pace in the chase group, but I know it was around the halfway mark. It felt odd to be so far back and running so poorly considering how well my training had gone. In my previous Boston Marathons, I had finished third, fourth, and fourth, and I had run up front through most of the race. Now, it became painfully clear that this would not be my day, but I still felt a glimmer of hope—not for myself but for Meb. Though I would certainly be envious if he crossed the finishing line first, it would feel like a victory for me and for America. I recall going up and over the legendary Heartbreak Hill at mile twenty and yelling to a spectator, "How is Meb doing?" They told me he was still winning the race when he'd passed by. A small smile crept across my face. I knew that if Meb had made it over Heartbreak in the lead, he stood a good chance of winning.

Meb had to fight hard all the way to the finish, but he managed to hold off a fast-closing Wilson Chebet of Kenya, recording arguably the most memorable win in the history of the storied Boston Marathon. I crossed the finishing line much, much later in what was my worst marathon performance ever. To this day, I couldn't tell you what my time was because I never bothered to look at the clock when I finished or even cared to look up the results after the race. Walking through the finishing chute, I was disappointed in my performance, but despite this I desperately wanted to know how Meb had done. I asked volunteer after volunteer whether Meb had won, but nobody was able to answer. I finally heard confirmation that he had indeed won.

I share this story not to take credit for Meb's win. Meb had to run his heart out that day, and he deserves full credit for winning the race. I'm sharing this story because that day I realized that sometimes the biggest victories we experience are not our own. They are victories we can share in because we played a part in someone's win by encouraging them and supporting them. It can be hard to take joy in another person's victory—especially if we wanted that victory for ourselves— but I have found that I can take joy in someone else's triumph if I can look at the bigger picture and see my role as part of a collective. I didn't win the Boston Marathon that day, but an American did, and so as an American, I could celebrate that victory as if it were my own.

I'm sure you can think of moments when you've contributed to, invested in, or helped someone on their journey, then watched them become victorious. As a coach, I experience this a lot more than I did when I was competing. I find that watching those I love and have invested in achieve their goals is much more fulfilling than any of my own achievements. It's hard to articulate the feeling, but perhaps the best way for me to say it is that when we partake in the victories of others, it shows us that we are part of something greater than ourselves, which is tremendously gratifying.

You can probably tell by now that I spend a lot of time thinking about my definition of success. I feel it's important to examine it regularly to open my mind to definitions that are different from what I've been told or am being told by the world, and I like to look for definitions that are more in line with my beliefs. My definition of success is deep and multifaceted, but taking part in the victories of others and participating in something bigger than myself are large parts of it. When my view of success is so small that it's all about me and my performance, my life is deeply unfulfilling. But when I open up my definition to include the success of others and the collective, I'm much more satisfied. Rick Warren says in his memorable opening sentence of *The Purpose Driven Life*, "It's not about you." I think these words resonate so strongly with me and many others because we all know how fulfilling it is to be part of something. I felt this in a tremendous way at the 2014 Boston Marathon, which will forever mark me, as well as many others, for a number of reasons, but one of the biggest is that what I was part of was hugely important for our country.

Seasons

In the fall of 2015, I was sitting in an airplane and staring out the window, frustrated with where I was in my running. It had been four years since I had come down with plantar fasciitis and battled through the ensuing injuries. I hadn't run a good marathon since the 2012 Olympic Trials, and my body was showing me sign after sign that it had given me everything it could during my twenty years of running. My main symptom at this point was extreme fatigue. It seemed that no matter how I tweaked my training, my nutrition, or my weight, nothing was getting my body to function properly again. Many times I left my house full of optimism only to run for fifteen minutes before my body felt so tired I was forced to walk back. The only way I can describe it is that I felt like I was slowly melting into the ground with every step. It was a horrible feeling and made running not very much fun. It took me four years to figure out it was time to stop, because I had to explore every possible training approach I could think of to see if one would work. I knew I had to leave no stone unturned before deciding it was time to quit; otherwise I knew I would be up at night thinking, *If only I'd tried . . .*

I'd always known this moment would come, and I knew that it would hurt to hang up my running shoes, but that didn't help with the frustration I was feeling.

As I stared out the window, I prayed for comfort. And I felt God answer, "It was never meant to last forever." I love how God can speak such short, simple truths that bring healing to the deepest part of our hearts. I let out a huge sigh of relief. It wasn't that I had messed up my running career, although I'm sure I made plenty of mistakes. The reality is that professional athletics isn't meant to last forever for anyone. As I thought about it, I realized that most beautiful things in life aren't meant to last forever. Sunrises are special because they last but a moment. Each day is precious because it must end. This truth allowed me to appreciate my running career for what it was—a beautiful season that gave me many extraordinary experiences and taught me lessons that would shape me for the rest of my life. But it had become clear that this season was over and a new season was beginning. I think what I felt at the end of my running career wasn't as much frustration as it was shame—shame that I had messed things up. God's words to me that it wasn't meant to last forever encouraged me to realize that even though I hadn't done everything perfectly, sometimes seasons just end because there is an ending point. Once I was able to remove the shame, I was able to find peace to transition to the next season.

A few months later, I announced my retirement from professional running, which wasn't an emotionally hard thing for me to do. Even with the release of the *New York Times* feature story on my retirement and the well-wishes from fans, I never really got emotional—not because I didn't care but because God had already dealt with my heart and I felt nothing but peace and excitement for the new season. But I remember that on the day the news broke that I was retiring, there was one emotional moment. Asics put together a touching video reflecting on my career and giving other pro runners the opportunity to wish me well, but I didn't get the chance to watch it (it was released in the morning) till after I picked up my girls from school in the afternoon. We pulled into a gas station, and while waiting for the tank to fill, I finally pulled up the video and watched it. I was glad it was dark out because I think it was the only time my girls have seen me cry, but I was able to hide it from them pretty well. (Not that I pride myself on that—I wish I was a little more emotional at times.) What touched me in the video was the people who wished me well, like Sara, Meb, Deena, Joe Vigil, Bob Larsen, and others, because they were people whom I had traveled the road with, had been through war with, and I knew I would miss that. The other part of the video that brought tears to my eyes was a brief clip that showed our Siberian husky, Kai, sprinting through the forest in full flight, legs eating up the ground beneath her. Even as I write this, just thinking of that clip moves me to tears, which might sound random to you, or maybe it doesn't—I don't know. But for me watching Kai flying through the air triggered a response in my body that said, "I know what that feels like, and it feels so, so, so good." I miss those moments. I miss flying effortlessly through the forest with no one but God watching. I miss the beautiful sensation of being out on a run and having it click, making it feel effortless. Those days were few for me, but they marked me forever.

After my retirement, my focus shifted from developing my talent as a runner to being a good husband to Sara and a good father to our newly adopted daughters. I had also picked up the hobby of weightlifting, which I found comical considering that during my running days, I hated to lift—in part because I was incredibly weak. I often tell people that when I was a professional runner, I would get a sore shoulder from stirring chili. I began weightlifting with a lot of research. I bought Arnold Schwarzenegger's bodybuilding book, read a ton of articles, and watched YouTube videos whenever I had the chance. I had a lot to learn about technique. Because I was so tight from running, I had a hard time getting into the proper positions, especially for deadlifting and squatting. I remember reading an entire book on how to squat, which helped me to do a butt-to-the-ground squat for the first time in my life. I was on a bit of a lone journey when it came to weights, but I was loving it.

When I started lifting, I couldn't bench press my weight, which was only 140 pounds. My squat and deadlift were not much better, so as you can imagine, being a former Olympic athlete, I felt more than a little self-conscious walking around in the weight room as the weakest person in the gym. Even guys who looked super unfit could lift three times what I was lifting. But something shifted within me and, as I'd done with running decades before, I began to love what I had hated. What I love about lifting is that you can go hard every day— you simply change the part of the body that you're hitting. I typically work chest and back one day, arms the next day, then legs the last day of the cycle. Rinse and repeat, but always changing up the workout slightly to provide new stimulus.

I also loved lifting because I was finally seeing a return on my investment of time and energy. I'd been spinning my wheels for the last four years trying to get back into the running shape I'd been in before injury. Yet no matter how hard I worked, my body wouldn't respond. After four years of seeing no results, it was clear that I'd never get back to where I'd been, and my mission felt complete. I had fulfilled my vision. I had run with the best runners in the world, and I had helped others through my running. I felt like I had done a good job harvesting the running talent God had given me and had fulfilled my potential, but now that season was over. Yet I was still the same person. I still loved to push myself physically every day, just not by running. Weightlifting filled that need. This was hugely important for me, allowing me to transition into my next season of life and stay true to who I am.

It was fun to see such remarkable growth in my strength and size once I started weightlifting. I quickly put on twenty pounds—most of which, but certainly not all, was muscle—and increased my strength significantly. I still didn't consider myself big or strong, but I loved seeing the improvement I was making. I felt like I was conducting my own mad scientist experiment of nature versus nurture. One would think that a 2:04 marathon runner would not have the genetics to get very big or strong, but I have always felt like nurture plays a bigger role than nature. This was a way to test my thinking. Three years ago today, as I write, I was 127 pounds at five foot ten and had a hard time moving any weight at all. I actually pulled a rib out of place doing a core exercise. Not sure how one does that, but that's how weak I was. Today, I'm 180 pounds and can bench 310, deadlift 405, and squat 365. Those numbers aren't going to win any weightlifting competitions (the world record in the deadlift is 1,181 pounds), but they're not bad considering my genetics and history with running. I think the answer to my experiment is that nurture (training) can get you a long way in any area of life—perhaps getting you into the top tenth percentile in any category—but if you are going to be a world beater, you absolutely must have the genetics to go with it.

It has been interesting to compare training for weightlifting with training for running, because I have found them to be similar. Many of the principles I learned to train for running are also used in weightlifting, and vice versa. One example is progressive loading, which is the idea that you must continue to put more and more weight on the bar. It sounds obvious and elementary, but it's actually hard to do and takes creativity and ingenuity to accomplish. It's easy to walk into the weight room, throw on the same weight as usual, and do the same routine, but it usually results in little gains. The key to breakthrough is to keep increasing the amount of resistance. The same is true for running. Just last night, I was talking to Sara about her marathon training and how we can continue to "add weight to the bar," because I know this is the only way to maximize her potential. She must keep pushing herself in new ways to get different results. I say all that just to illustrate what I've found to be true about moving from season to season. Often, lessons we learned in one season are meant to help us in future seasons, so even if you are coming out of a rough season, take solace in the fact that it was not a waste. The lessons you learned through your trials will help you on your journey in this new season.

My favorite passage about appreciating all the seasons in life is a famous one found in Ecclesiastes 3 (vv. 1–8):

There is an appointed time for everything. And there is a time for every event under heaven—

A time to give birth and a time to die;
A time to plant and a time to uproot what is planted.
A time to kill and a time to heal;
A time to tear down and a time to build up.

A time to weep and a time to laugh;
A time to mourn and a time to dance.
A time to throw stones and a time to gather stones;
A time to embrace and a time to shun embracing.
A time to search and a time to give up as lost;
A time to keep and a time to throw away.
A time to tear apart and a time to sew together;
A time to be silent and a time to speak.
A time to love and a time to hate;
A time for war and a time for peace.

I love this passage because it captures what I experienced in my transition from running—that nothing is meant to last forever and that we must be able to identify the end of one season so we can enter the new season. Things can get confusing, hard, and frustrating for us whenever we try to drag one season into another. We are meant to carry with us the lessons we learn, but we must keep moving forward to find new ground.

Consistency

One day after my running career had come to a close, I was working out on the toe-raise machine when I got a text message from my friend Matthew Barnett, pastor of the Dream Center in Los Angeles. Pastor Matthew is a runner, and I'd spoken at his amazing church, which serves the less fortunate on the streets and in the communities of LA. PM (as I like to refer to him) told me that he'd just signed up for this crazy race, the World Marathon Challenge, in which he would run seven marathons in seven consecutive days on seven continents. Hearing about this epic challenge made something jump inside of me, much like what happened when I was thirteen years old and had been given the vision to run around Big Bear Lake. It seemed odd to me that I thought I would love to do that, considering that at the time, I was running only three days a week and only to keep Sara company on her training runs. I had zero desire to go for a run on my own, yet the description of the Challenge combined with the knowledge that PM was doing the race to raise support for his church drew me in. I spent a few moments debating how I should respond, then texted him back saying that if he wanted company, I'd love to go on the trip with him. To my surprise, he invited me to join him. After my shock at how quickly this was all happening, the reality of running seven marathons in seven days on seven continents sank in. When I was running professionally, I'd never trained even close to how many miles (183.4) I'd have to run that week. Plus I was retired from professional running. Being thirty pounds heavier and running only fifteen miles a week compared with 120 miles a week during my pro days, running just one marathon would certainly feel a lot different. But seven marathons? This was going to be an epic challenge!

I started training for the World Marathon Challenge the summer before our January 2017 start. I added more and more miles and even started pacing Sara in some of her workouts and races. Unfortunately, it wasn't more than a couple of months before I felt the same fatigue I'd felt prior to my retirement. Once again, running was teaching me a valuable lesson: if in a new season you try to do what you've done in a previous season, it's not likely to work. I decided then that I would rather enjoy my life and have one rough week of running instead of hating my life for three months of training beyond what my body could—or wanted to—do.

I ran three days a week, mostly three- to four-mile runs with an occasional "long" run of eight miles. Not typical training even for a novice runner attempting their first half marathon, let alone someone attempting to run seven marathons in a row. To make things even more difficult, I was lifting hard every day and continuing to get bigger and stronger. By the start of the World Marathon Challenge, I weighed close to 180 lbs and my max bench press was more than 200 pounds and my squat and deadlift were more than 300 pounds. I was working hard and enjoying life, but I wasn't running a whole lot. I kind of relished the idea of not training. In my mind, anyone could do the Challenge if they trained for it, but where was the challenge in that? If you didn't train for it, that would be a true challenge.

I departed Redding almost a week before our first marathon. It was quite a journey down to Chile for our briefing before leaving for our first destination, Antarctica. I had two back-to-back red-eye flights as I ventured to South America for the first time in my life. Long layovers in San Salvador, Lima, and Santiago gave me the opportunity to explore new cities, which I love to do. One of the aspects of being a professional runner I'd enjoyed the most was the traveling. Growing up as one of five kids, all supported by my dad's teaching salary, we didn't have the money to fly around the country, much less the world. But when I started to fly to big track meets as a junior in high school, I felt like a whole new world was opening up to me. It forever ignited my travel itch.

I finally arrived in the southernmost tip of Chile, where I spent two nights and had several briefings before leaving for Antarctica. It was surreal sitting in those briefings and feeling the full weight of what we were about to do. When I met the other competitors (there were about forty other runners), I knew it was going to be a fun week, no matter how many miles I'd be slogging through. I was surprised that most of the runners seemed like normal people. Given the magnitude of the Challenge, I'd anticipated being on a trip with a bunch of crazy runners who spent most of their time running, reading about running, and watching running documentaries. This wasn't the case at all. The group was filled with a variety of individuals, each with their own inspirational story. There was everyone from successful businesspeople who loved to take on running challenges to war vets who were competing despite physical handicaps incurred during their service to one runner bravely battling brain cancer. The best runner on the trip was Mike Wardian. I'd raced Mike at the 2007 Olympic Marathon Trials, where he led for a good amount of the race early on. Mike is one of the rare individuals who can race fast over and over with little rest between races. To give you an idea of what I am talking about, I typically ran only two marathons a year, as is customary among professional runners, whereas Mike would run a marathon, then hop on a plane to another city to race again that night. I knew Mike was going to crush this challenge because it seemed designed for him. We once had been competitors, but now we were simply friends.

When we finally left for Antarctica, we boarded the most archaic airplane I'd ever been on. It was this massive old Russian airplane built to endure extreme conditions. It was also able to land on ice, which was important because we'd be flying into Union Glacier and touching down on ice hundreds of feet thick. As we boarded the plane, we resembled astronauts in our oversized, super-thick pants and massive red jackets that looked like they could endure negative-hundred-degree temperatures. The outfits seemed like overkill, but we were assured we would be glad to have the warmth when we stepped off the plane in Antarctica. In addition, there was limited heat on the plane, so we needed to dress accordingly. The plane looked like something out of a 1950s movie. Inside, various wires and cords hung down from the ceiling, and a musty smell fit perfectly with the vibe. The only form of entertainment we had for the four-hour flight was a big screen on which an old movie was playing. Most of us, though, passed the time talking about what Antarctica would be like and speculating on how it would feel to land on a sheet of ice. On our descent into Union Glacier, a live camera shot was projected from the front of the airplane onto the movie screen so we could watch our landing. I'll never forget seeing the blue ice coming into the frame as I braced myself for what was sure to be the scariest landing I'd ever experienced, but it was just the opposite. The landing was so smooth that I couldn't even feel when we touched down. It was incredible.

When the door of the plane opened, I was expecting to get hit by the coldest wave of air I'd ever felt in my life, but again I was surprised when it didn't feel any different from a normal winter day in Mammoth Lakes. I was overheating in my astronaut costume, and I quickly ripped off my huge jacket so that I was wearing only a T-shirt. We had arrived on the perfect day. The sun was shining, as it would all day. (It was summer in Antarctica, so the sun simply circled around the sky, making it impossible to tell what time of day it was.) I hesitated to take my first step onto the ice, certain I'd fall flat on my back, but it had a grippy texture that made it fun to walk on. We all meandered around for a bit, snapping photos and taking videos, before loading into the coolest SUVs outfitted with giant snow tires. The six-mile ride to our group camp was super bumpy, causing us to hit our heads on the vehicle ceilings on more than one occasion. We were all laughing hysterically as if we were on a ride in Disneyland.

When we arrived at our base camp, the sun was blazing. I was sweating it out in all my clothes, despite brisk temperatures in the single digits. The radiant sun made it seem much warmer. We were being hit from sunlight above as well as bouncing off the snow and ice. We would be at base camp for a couple of days, with the option of starting our marathon on the third day, weather permitting. We passed the time taking in long meals, getting to know each others' stories, and deepening our friendships. Even though it was just a temporary camp, the food was amazing. Every meal was a full spread with something for every diet. I still don't know how they managed to get such incredible food all the way down there, but we were all impressed by the quality of the meals coming out of the kitchen.

We weren't allowed to leave camp for those three days, except to do our tune-up runs. We'd be running on a groomed six-mile loop that was pancake flat and felt great to run on. It was the softest surface we would have all week—the rest of the marathons were held mostly on concrete paths. (Concrete is way harder than asphalt, so I typically avoided it at all costs to minimize the pounding in my legs.) It felt good to run on the snow again. I'd run on snow a lot in Mammoth, and then again when I moved to Flagstaff. I'd always been around snow since the time we moved to Big Bear when I was five years old. I felt strangely at home on what seemed like a different planet.

Before the trip, I was planning how I was going to fit in my daily lifting sessions during the week. I had worked hard for more than a year to add a lot of muscle and strength, and I wasn't about to allow one week away to set me back. I had heard we would get day hotels wherever we raced so that we had time after the marathon to shower before getting back on the plane to travel to our next location. I figured most of these hotels would have gyms or fitness centers I could use, but I also knew that hitting the weights in Antarctica would be a challenge. I was right about that—there was not a weight to be seen at our camp. But instead of looking at the situation as a chance to take some time off, I instead saw it as an opportunity to get creative and add some variety to my sessions. I always told the kids I coached on the high school cross-country team to find an excuse to run no matter what—meaning, don't miss. Consistency is one of our most powerful tools, but it can work for us or against us, depending on what we're being consistent about.

When I'm gymless on the road, I set the timer on my watch and tell myself that I'm going to work out for an hour, no matter what. To keep my workout moving, I like to take exactly forty-five seconds rest between exercises to make sure I'm not wasting time. In Antarctica, I noticed that the tents were held up by some strong pipes. Where some people see pipes, I see a pullup bar. One day I did supersets of pushups and pullups with forty-five seconds of rest for an hour straight. I did pushups a variety of ways (close grip, V pushups, decline pushups, explosive pushups, etc.) and alternated between chinups and pullups. The next day, I hit my arms by curling heavy bottles of cooking oil or whatever other heavy objects I could find. I was able to perform a variety of biceps, triceps, and shoulder exercises, which gave me a nice arm workout.

Over a long dinner the night before the first race, we made friendly bets about what times we thought we could run in the snow and cold for our first marathon. Although Mike was the only one gunning for fast times, the group also included some very fit runners who could consistently run a marathon at or below three hours. I arranged a bet that if Mike ran under 2:45, then Jon, one of the other competitors who attended PM's church and whom I eventually became friends with, would arrange a wine-tasting weekend in Napa for Mike, Pastor Matthew, me, and our wives. It was nice to have a little extra motivation for that first marathon. We figured that Mike would have to average 6:17 per mile to run under 2:45, and I decided to help him if I could by leading and letting him tuck in behind me. I hadn't run even one mile at that pace for four months, but I was hoping some residual running fitness might allow me to help him for a few miles.

By the third day, we all had played enough Jenga and cards and done enough reading to last us for the entire adventure, and we were eager to get running. Luckily, when we awoke in our two-man tents after another restless night (it was challenging to get quality sleep when it was light outside twenty-four hours a day), we learned that the weather would be good enough for us to run our first marathon. We made our way to the starting line before the race director—and amazing all-around person—Richard Donovan said the words I would be less and less excited to hear as the week wore on: "Three, two, one, run!"

Taking those first steps felt both significant and insignificant at the same time. The obvious significance of it was that we were embarking on the adventure and challenge of a lifetime. The insignificance of it was that they were only the first few steps of what I guessed would be around fifty thousand for the first marathon alone. Speaking again about consistency, it's easy to justify skipping just one workout or eating just one cookie, because the truth is that it won't kill you—but the mentality will. The "just this once" mentality can turn one missed workout into a week of missed workouts, which can stretch into a month, a year, or even a lifetime. Taking one step seems like such a small part of such a long journey, but that one step means everything because it sets you on the path of success, and success is made up of a million little steps in the right direction.

In those first steps, I quickly realized that pacing Mike was not going to happen. It wasn't so much that I was breathing hard, frozen solid, and carrying around extra pounds as it was that my legs just weren't used to moving fast anymore. It wasn't in the cards for me, even though this pace would have felt like jogging in the prime of my running career. It goes to show that it doesn't matter who you are or what you've accomplished, if you try to race at a pace you haven't prepared for, it isn't going to happen.

I was fine to let Mike go, knowing that I was sure to die a long, slow death. The weather was good, with the temperatures feeling the same as on many of the days I'd run in the winters in Mammoth. I was dressed in thin racing tights, a thin long-sleeved shirt, and a light running jacket, along with my beanie and gloves. I felt comfortable the entire way. I even had to unzip my jacket at times to make sure I didn't start sweating. Sweating is what you want to avoid in Antarctica, because sweat that freezes can quickly cause hypothermia and worse.

I enjoy a lot of things about being retired from professional running, and one of the biggest things is being able to listen to music while racing. As a pro, I always listened to music when training on my own, but I could never listen to music in races because the rules prohibited it. It was nice to have some tunes along for the seven-marathon journey. I played music on the phone I carried in my jacket pocket. I'd just downloaded the newest album by Housefires, which is incredible worship music that will forever bring me back to my week of traveling and running around the world. I listened to that album every day for three, four, or even five hours, depending on how long it took me to complete each marathon.

I was in a great mood during that first 10K loop and was still in second place, but that didn't last long. Every loop, I got about fifty seconds per mile slower. I think this had a lot to do with my fueling strategy. Because I was determined not to lose weight on this trip, I had packed nearly a hundred protein bars. For the first marathon, I ate two protein bars every 10K, which amounted to about forty grams of protein every forty-five to fifty minutes. I quickly learned that while my stomach was digesting all the protein, my muscles were screaming for carbohydrates. By the last lap, I was dying hard and had faded into about seventh position. Lucky for me, at mile twenty-three, I reached an unmanned tent set up as an aid station that had been stocked with dried fruit, candy, cookies, and other quick carbs. I felt like a kid on Halloween! I gingerly got on my knees and crawled into the tent, grabbing as many cookies and candies as I could hold, and started inhaling them like I hadn't eaten in forty days. Sugar had never tasted so good, and I felt my mind functioning again. I survived those last three miles, but it wasn't pretty. The kicker for me was when a guy who had never run a marathon before passed me toward the end of the race. He had just completed a multi-month, cross-country ski from Union Glacier to the South Pole and back, and he'd decided to hop into the marathon on a whim. I was definitely humbled at that point, but my time (3:26:31) was still where I wanted it to be, and I had crossed marathon number one off the list. I tried not to think about the fact that I had to run another marathon in twenty-four hours as I headed first to the food tent to pound some more food and then to the "workout" tent to get in my hour of upper body strengthening. That week, my daily hourlong lifts were my dessert at the end of the meal, my reward for slogging through the marathons.

It wasn't long after I finished my workout of pullups and pushups that we boarded our old Russian plane for the four-hour journey back to Chile. I was looking forward to getting some sleep, because this was just one out of two opportunities we would have to sleep in a hotel overnight. The next morning, the sun seemed to come up way too soon. I put down a couple of Starbucks Via packets and slammed a few Muscle Milk protein bars before heading to the start of marathon number two. It was strange showing up to a "race" so casually. Back when I was competing, I always drank a shake for breakfast (to avoid an upset stomach) two hours and thirty minutes before the start of the race, waited to drink my coffee until ninety minutes before the race, and then began my fifteen- to twenty-minute warmup, followed by drills and strides exactly sixty minutes before the race. Everything was always fine-tuned and timed to the minute. But now it was refreshing just to roll out of bed, have some coffee, and eat some fun food, such as protein bars, before running a marathon with no real concern for timing. At the speeds I was running—anywhere from one to three hours slower than my marathon personal best—I certainly didn't need to warm up.

The marathon in Chile ran along the Pacific Ocean the entire way. It was a beautiful out-and-back course. It felt odd to run on hard cement after running on soft snow for three days. Luckily, I had opted to run all week long in the cushiest shoes Asics had available. I knew the repeated pounding on my body, especially with the extra weight I was carrying, would be one of the most significant challenges of the trip. I felt super stiff during the first couple of miles of that second marathon, but I was surprised to discover that my legs woke up after that, and I ended up feeling pretty similar strength-wise to the first marathon. I wouldn't say I crushed it, but the race went way better than expected, and I finished in 3:06:33, which was faster than I thought I could run considering my light training before the competition.

It felt good to board our private jet in Chile, which had all business-class seats, after our ride on the Russian warplane.

I had never been on a private jet before, so I was wide-eyed on that flight. After the second marathon, I was feeling a lot better about life. Yes, I was sore and stiff and had difficultly sitting down and getting up, but I'd done something I'd never done before—two back-to-back marathons. This was an important lesson for me: often, our biggest challenges are in our minds. My body was more than capable of running seven marathons in seven days on seven continents, even with the lack of training, but my mind took some convincing. After I finished that second marathon, though, I knew I could do it. All I had to do was keep putting one foot in front of the other and not think about how long or how hard the journey would be. I couldn't be concerned about all the steps it would take to complete my week of running. I only needed to concern myself with consistently taking a step in the right direction.

Closure

With each marathon, the anticipation of crossing the final finishing line in Sydney was slowly building. I tried not to think about it because I knew that if I focused on the finish, I could get overwhelmed by how far I had to go. The closer I got to the final line, the more I had to stay present and focus on running the mile I was in. But I was still having a great time on the trip, enjoying every conversation and loving traveling the globe.

I had been looking forward to the third of the seven marathons, which was in Miami. It would feel good to be back on US soil, and some friends were planning to join me for a few miles of the race. The flight from southern Chile to Miami wasn't long enough for me. I wished we could have circled the globe, sleeping the entire way, before having to run again. This became the theme of the week. I do a lot of traveling, and I'm always happy when the plane touches down wherever my destination may be, but that week I didn't want any of the flights to end. The longer the flight, the better, as far as I was concerned. Before the trip, when I thought of all the flying we'd be doing, I imagined I might set a Guinness world record for the most movies watched in a week, but I didn't watch a single one. I spent all of my time on the plane either eating or sleeping. I can't imagine having done the trip on a commercial airliner in economy seating. Being able to lie down flat was a game changer. I figured business class must have been invented especially for this challenge.

Getting off the plane in Miami on wobbly legs, I had no idea what to expect. To be honest, I was trying not to expect anything. I always remember what my coach, Terrance Mahon, told me is a good mindset to take to the starting line of a marathon: "Adopt the saying of the Samurai: 'expect nothing, be ready for everything.'" Miami, even in the winter, was way warmer than I preferred for running. I think the temperatures were in the seventies, but for elite marathoners, that's super hot. The ideal temperature varies from athlete to athlete, but it's typically in the range of forty to fifty-five degrees.

My plan for marathons has always been the same: go out hard and give God a chance. I've had God show up in some incredible ways during my races, and I always want to give Him a chance to strengthen me. I like to think that if you don't start out at a pace that's beyond what you're capable of, you don't need to ask God to step in and give you extra strength. God shows up when we take risks, whether it's praying for someone, engaging someone in a conversation about faith, moving to the other side of the planet, or going out faster than you should in a marathon. My faith beckons me to push myself beyond my limits. I also like to say that it's proven by science that an object in motion likes to stay in motion, so why not make that motion fast and try to hold it? To me, this seems a lot easier than being twenty-four miles into a race and then trying to pick up the pace. This is the opposite of what 99 percent of marathon coaches will tell you, but I believe that sometimes you have to risk it all to gain it all.

During the Challenge, I tried to start my marathons as close to a three-hour-marathon pace as possible and then end up running somewhere in the 3:04 to 3:50 range. Miami was no different. I suffered through those last few three-mile out-and-backs and was happy to arrive at the finishing line in 3:15:38. After another gym session and a quick lunch, it was time to board our flight to Madrid.

In 2011, I met a friend, Jaap, at our church's School of Supernatural Ministry when Sara and I were auditing classes there prior to the 2012 Olympic Marathon Trials. Jaap was from Holland and was a serious cyclist. We quickly became friends, and he often paced me on his bike for my workouts leading up to the Trials. Jaap had moved back to Holland after spending a few years in Redding, but we always made an effort to get together whenever Sara raced in Europe. Jaap agreed to meet me in Madrid to bike alongside me in my fourth marathon.

I'm so grateful Jaap was there that day, because it was one of the worst runs I'd ever had in my life. Having my friend there to joke with, talk to, and vent my frustration to allowed me to get through a brutal marathon, a race in which I felt like I had a thick layer of molasses on the bottoms of my shoes. I'm still not sure why I felt so horrid—maybe it was because of the three marathons I had just run or the travel without a full night's sleep—but that's running in a nutshell. Some days you feel amazing and don't understand why, while other days you feel terrible and don't know why. The tricky thing about trying to understand performance in running is that there are so many variables—sleep, nutrition, hydration, training cycles, temperature, equipment, and so on—all of which are hard to independently isolate, making it difficult to understand what is causing things to go either right or wrong. For me, nutrition has always played a major part in my performance. When we were in Antarctica, I was talking with Peter, a Canadian runner who was also doing the Challenge, and he told me that his coach warned him this wouldn't be a running competition. It would be an eating competition. Peter's coach knew that proper fueling would be critical to getting through the endless miles. After Antarctica, I abandoned my high-protein strategy and went straight to the sugar. I always tell my kids that the only time it's healthy to eat sugar is while you're running or after a hard workout, because your muscles are depleted of glucose and open to receiving carbohydrates. If you eat sugar when you aren't in this state, the likelihood of its going to fat is high. During that week, I probably ate more sugar than I'd eaten in the previous five years. Most photos of me that week show me cramming cookies, donuts, and candy into my mouth as I ran. I had challenged other runners on the trip to try to out-eat me, but it was clear before the end of the week that I had won the eating competition. Despite stuffing my face, I was still down nearly ten pounds by the time I returned home.

People often ask me what was my all-time favorite marathon, and the answer is usually whatever race I felt the best in. Running in Spain that day should have been an amazing experience. We were running on a nice, cool winter day through a beautiful park, and I had Jaap there to keep me company, but I recall the pain that plagued me from start to finish. I even remember at one point venting to Jaap, "I hate running!" I can't tell you how many times I've said that in my career. Sometimes it just needs to be said so I can feel sane again. I think it's okay to vent—you just have to choose wisely to whom and where you do it. I think one of the greatest challenges professional athletes face is suffering a heartbreaking performance and then, before they even have time to catch their breath, much less manage their disappointment, they have reporters sticking microphones in their faces and asking pointed questions. Or they have a pack of kids swarming them, excited to take a picture together or get an autograph, which can be hard to deal with when an athlete is feeling down. But that's part of the job for professionals. They must learn to carry themselves well, whether in victory or in defeat.

My marathon time in Spain was 3:41:41, and that was everything I had that day. I had nothing left at the end of the race. Jaap and I completed a gym session, and when it came time to say goodbye, I could see the concern in his eyes. Jaap knew that the worst of my suffering probably wasn't behind me. I took solace in his concern, knowing that he understood what it feels like to physically suffer. I also realized that while my suffering seemed extreme, other runners on this trip were experiencing a lot worse. I was on the trip to support Pastor Matthew, and I was sincerely trying to do this, but I think he helped me more than I helped him. In Spain, PM had a nasty knee injury—we learned later that he had torn something— that caused him to limp, jog, and walk the last four marathons. I was inspired by his ability to keep moving forward, despite being hit with a huge setback. PM maintained a good attitude and served as a powerful example of how to persevere and suffer well. Every time we passed each other, I gave him a holler and a fist pump because I could see the gritty determination on his face. He inspired me to follow his example of suffering with grace and strength.

After the sufferfest in Spain, we landed in Morocco after a fairly short flight. Richard, the race director, was considering having us run as soon as we arrived that night, then get some sleep in the hotel after the race. The thought of doing another marathon that same day—especially after the horrid race I'd just run—made me nauseated. It may seem normal to ultra-marathoners to run two marathons in a day, but for me a three-mile cooldown after a marathon felt like an eternity. I couldn't imagine running another 26.2 miles so soon. I was relieved when Richard decided that we would sleep for about five hours before running bright and early the next morning.

I didn't know what to expect for marathon number five in Morocco. If it was anything like the previous marathon, I was in for a long, long day. On the starting line, I reminded myself what God had taught me along my running journey: yesterday doesn't matter; the only thing that matters is the here and now. I did start out more conservatively in Morocco, because my legs were sorer than they had ever been and my energy felt like it was seriously declining in those first few miles, but I was surprised to feel better as the race went on. Before I knew it, I was running at a six-minutes-per-mile pace. I was shocked. I knew the night's sleep had helped, but I also felt like I was starting to train myself back into running shape. I was so undertrained going into the Challenge that I was getting fitter with each marathon.

What I remember best about marathon number five was the feeling I had in my spirit. I felt like a warrior out there. I kept telling myself, *Not today*, which meant, "I'm not backing down today. I'm giving it everything I have. I'm winning this battle." I was fighting a personal battle out there, and it didn't matter that I was running an hour slower than my marathon best. I still had the same sensation that my spirit was rising up within me to fight. I loved the feeling.

A few other times during the week, I experienced the

sensations I'd felt when racing professionally. This is what is so special about running. It doesn't matter how fast or how slow you're going, all the runners in a race get to share similar experiences. I think this is what makes the running community so tight-knit. We understand what we're all going through, regardless of level.

Morocco ended up being my fastest marathon of the seven (3:04:56), and my confidence soared. After that race, my goal changed from survival to getting faster the next two days. I was excited to race again in Dubai. After my weightlifting session, Mike Wardian and I walked to a nearby restaurant to get some food before boarding our plane. Mike noticed I was limping slightly and commented on it. I had felt a small twinge of pain in my hip after I'd finished the race that day, but I shook it off as normal postmarathon pain. It was just a five out of ten on my pain tolerance scale, so I wasn't at all worried about it.

I felt pretty well rested from the somewhat long flight from Morocco to Dubai. I wasn't stoked about the warm and humid conditions, but we were on day six and I was getting stronger. With only two marathons remaining, I felt I was on the homestretch of this epic challenge. I was hoping I could break three hours in both Dubai and Sydney. I started out much faster this time in Dubai, feeling pretty good in the opening 10K. We were running on a really cool rubber track surface that ran right along the beach. It was much softer than our typical concrete courses, which I was thankful for. Early in the race, I noticed my hip pain, and it became increasingly sharp as the race went on. I tried not to think about it because I've learned that often the more I focus on the pain, the more intense it feels. Case in point: my daughter Jasmine cries whenever her sisters braid her hair, but if we put a movie on, she is fine and doesn't shed a tear. I decided to focus on the beautiful surroundings in Dubai and appreciate how blessed I was to experience such an epic challenge with Pastor Matthew and the rest of the runners and staff, but my stride began to change, and by mile twenty I was limping noticeably and had to resort to walking some stretches. I still ran 3:46:20, but my last half was terribly slow. I must have run more than two hours the last half marathon, but I made it. Despite my hip pain blossoming into a full-blown injury, I knew that I had only one marathon left and that, one way or another, I would make it to the finishing line.

The trip to Sydney seemed to fly by (as flights tend to do when you are asleep). I wanted to stay on that plane for twenty more hours, but it was time to rally and move toward the starting line. I'll never forget standing up for the first time after the flight and taking a step. My leg nearly gave out and I winced as the pain took my breath away. I was hoping the hip would loosen up, but instead I felt the kind of pain I'd felt only once before—when I had a stress fracture in my sacrum. I was pretty sure I had a stress fracture in my hip. As I hobbled through the airport, I knew I was in for the longest marathon of my life.

Our seventh marathon in Sydney took place at Manly Beach. It was a beautiful stretch of concrete that, lucky for me, had grass next to it, which I opted to run on. There was no going out fast in this marathon. I was in the back from the beginning and pretty much stayed there, walking and limp-jogging on the mile-out, mile-back course. At one point, I stopped for a massage, hoping the massage therapist could work a miracle on my hip, but I knew that a massage wouldn't help a stress fracture. We started the race around 2:00 a.m., and I found solace in the peacefulness of the ocean waves crashing onto the beach and of the moon lighting our path.

Besides my hip injury, I was also concerned because when

we arrived in Sydney, Pastor Matthew had to be taken to the doctor. He had suffered the last three marathons, walking almost the entire way, but he had maintained the same inspiring, upbeat attitude he was known for in church. It spoke a lot to me that PM is always the same person, whether he's up on the stage or suffering through miles and miles of running in intense pain. I feel like it's easy to be inspired by great performances on the playing field, and rightfully so, but I am always more impressed by people who find joy, hope, and perseverance when they're in the middle of their worst day and suffering well. I was more inspired by PM on this trip than I was by watching Olympic athletes compete. He was a picture of what true success looks like. I was glad when I saw his smiling face as he ran through the warm night air in Sydney after the doctor cleared him to run. I caught him on one of the loops, and we ran and walked a number of miles together. We must have looked like quite the pair, gimping and grimacing our way up and down the beach path. If a non-runner had been watching us, they assuredly wouldn't have felt like lacing up their shoes for a run anytime soon.

Five hours and fifteen minutes after I'd started the marathon in Sydney, I finally made my way down the homestretch. Most of the other competitors had already finished, showered, and gotten something to eat, but some had stuck around to see me finish. There weren't a lot of fans watching that day as I limp-jogged across the finishing line for the very last time in my career in the marathon distance, but that didn't matter to me. This finishing line brought my marathon career full circle. Before the trip, I'd promised myself that the marathon in Sydney would be my last. I had always pictured ending my career on top, having one last great race and then, after finishing, kneeling down, taking off my running shoes, and leaving them on the finishing line. I would walk away barefoot, never looking back. I'd stolen the idea from wrestlers, who, at the end of their final match, take off their shoes and leave them on the mat. I'd always thought of that as a powerful act. It was a way of saying, "I gave it everything I had, there is nothing left, and now I am walking toward my next challenge." The problem with how my professional career had ended was that there *was* no last race. I was training for the 2016 Olympic Trials when my body gave me its final sign that it had had enough. Having no closing race with which to say goodbye to the sport wasn't how I'd pictured my career ending. Even though I didn't realize it until finishing my last marathon in Sydney, I still needed closure for my running career, and now I had the chance to do something about it. I thought it would be fitting to end it with something as epic as the World Marathon Challenge, since I'd started my career twenty-one years before with the epic challenge of running fifteen miles around Big Bear Lake. It felt like the circle had been completed. I had started with the vision of running with the best guys in the world and helping others, and I had done both of those things to the best of my ability. I had asked a lot of my body, and it had given me everything it could. Now it was time to give back and walk fully into my new season.

When I crossed the finishing line in Sydney, slowly and gingerly I got on my knees, took off my running shoes, and walked away in my socks, never looking back. I still don't know where those shoes are, but I heard that someone scooped them up as mementos. At the end of the week, my Fitbit stats were staggering. I had taken 308,727 steps, run and walked 211.7 miles, and averaged a daily burn of 5,755 calories. I took a screenshot of those stats, because I was sure I'd never come close to doing something like that again.

Limping back to our hotel, I was surprised to feel moved almost to the point of tears. I thought this was just supposed to be a symbolic act. I wasn't expecting to feel a whole lot of emotion from it. But I found that I had some sadness in saying goodbye to the marathon and to my professional running career. It was the same kind of sadness you feel when you lose a loved one with whom you've experienced life. You remember the good times, the hard times, and all the moments of life you've shared together. Running had taken me all around the world, had given me friendships, a wife, and a family, and had been a profession that rarely felt like a job. I was deeply grateful that God had given me the vision to run around Big Bear Lake when I was thirteen. I had no idea of the rewarding and fulfilling journey that awaited me, but it was clear that this journey was over.

What I've learned since the World Marathon Challenge is that for something to grow, something else usually has to die first. Humans live because plants and animals die. Seeds come from plants that die. In order for the sun to rise, it first has to set. I found that when I received the closure on my running that I'd been craving, I could move to my next season of life without trying to live in the past. From time to time, I still think about the ways I messed up in my running career and imagine what I might have done differently, and I try not to disregard those lessons because I believe that my mistakes can result in victory for others, but in the end, I remember that I did the very best I could with the knowledge I had. I ran with faith. I ran free. I ran hard. I ran fearless. This is what I am most proud of.

When something in your life dies—whether it be a job, a hobby, or a dream—I encourage you not to focus on what could have been and what is lost but instead to look for the new life and the new opportunities that result. A new season is here.

Victorious

A couple of nights ago, I was watching the finals of the women's halfpipe competition in the 2018 Winter Olympics. Chloe Kim was the favorite going in, and she did not disappoint. She posted such a high score (93.75 out of a possible 100) on her first of three runs that she had the gold medal clinched before she took her last run. When, as the last rider in the competition, Chloe stood at the top of the pipe, she knew she would be the Olympic gold medalist whether she had the best run of her life or the worst. She had zero pressure. She had already won.

Chloe went on to record one of her best performances ever on that run, earning a score of 98.25 and landing back-to-back 1080s. I can relate to the feeling Chloe must have had prior to that run. She must have felt incredibly light, free, and excited to see what would happen without any of the pressure that comes with competing. I understand how Chloe felt not because I was ever in the position of knowing I had already won but because I was able to develop this spirit toward the end of my career.

Early in my athletic life, I put so much pressure on myself

to perform well that sports actually weren't all that fun for me. This stronghold of the burden to perform well took a long time to be broken. It wasn't broken until I understood that in reality, I had already won, not because of anything I had done but because of what Jesus had already done for me. I realized that all I really wanted out of winning any level of athletic competition I already had within me. Was I seeking completeness? I was already complete. Was I seeking acceptance? I was already accepted. Was I seeking the elation that comes from doing something great? Greatness already dwells within me in the form of the Holy Spirit. Was I seeking wealth? My Dad already owns the entire universe. Was I seeking fame? My Dad is already the most famous person of all time. Was I seeking glory? My Dad will one day get all the glory of heaven and earth. I finally realized the simple truth that there is nothing I can possess that is more valuable nor is there anything I can accomplish that is greater than knowing God and being in a right relationship with Him. When the Holy Spirit comes and resides within all who have chosen to accept Jesus' free gift of salvation, we have received and achieved something far greater than anything we could ever experience on the playing field or at the finishing line. We have already won.

I would like to say that this was a one-time revelation and that once I realized this truth I never battled pressure again, but that wouldn't be true. I found that I had to daily decide to partner with that truth. I constantly had to tell myself, "I've already won," when I was on the starting line. To be honest, sometimes I still felt the pressure of performance, but it was the repeated action of declaring "I've already won" that became the reality I lived.

I remember walking into the 2012 Olympic Trials

technical meeting the night before the competition and feeling the tension, nerves, and tightness in the room. But I was in one of the best places I'd ever been spiritually. I felt light and free, like I had nothing to lose and everything to gain. The following day, I was so relaxed that I nearly missed the start of the race. This should have been my worst nightmare, because I had almost missed the start of the Olympic Trials. But this was the kind of lightness I was able to find, knowing that I had already won.

I like to imagine how Jesus would have competed in athletics, and this is what I am most struck by: He would be free. Yes, I also believe He would be able to push Himself harder than anyone ever has, but He wouldn't push Himself because He had to. He would push Himself because He was so motivated by His love for us and His love for the Father. Because He lacks nothing, He would be free to risk everything.

I know some people believe that performance pressure brings out the best in them, but I have to disagree. I always performed my best when I was free and light. My dad always used to tell me, "Happy feet make light feet." And what could make anyone happier than knowing they have already won?